LED ZEPPELIN
THE BOOK

LED ZEPPELIN
THE BOOK
CHRIS WELCH

PROTEUS BOOKS
London/New York

The author wishes to thank the following for their kind help, assistance and encouragement: Howard Mylett, Dave Lewis, Stewart Pearsall, Bill Harry, and the Adler typewriter company.

PROTEUS BOOKS is an imprint of
The Proteus Publishing Group

United States
PROTEUS PUBLISHING COMPANY, Inc.
9 West 57th Street, Suite 4503,
New York NY 10019

distributed by:
CHERRY LANE BOOKS COMPANY, Inc.
PO Box No 430,
Port Chester, NY 10573

United Kingdom
PROTEUS BOOKS LIMITED
Bremar House, Sale Place,
London W2 1PT

ISBN 0 86276 113 1 (Paperback)
ISBN 0 86276 114 X (Hardback)

First published in U.S. 1984
First published in U.K. 1984

Photo Credits: Andre Csillag, Barry Plummer, David Redfern,
Star File: Bob Gruen, Kate Simon, Chuck Pulin.
Barry Wentzell.

Editor: Mike Teasdale

Designed by: Adrian Hodgkins
Typeset by: SX Composing Ltd

Printed by Chanctonbury Press Ltd.
West Chiltington, Sussex

CONTENTS

One	Gotta Be Good Tonight	9
Two	Your Time is Gonna Come	22
Three	A Whole Lotta Love	37
Four	American Dreams	51
Five	Five Encores for Zeppelin	64
Six	Stairway To Heaven	77
Seven	Strange Days	88
Eight	The Song is Ended	110
Nine	Coda	126
Ten	The Zeppelin Treasure Hunt	138

TECHNICAL NOTES

Led Zeppelin's equipment became increasingly elaborate and more sophisticated over the years, but there remained various constants like John Bonham's allegiance to Ludwig drums. The following list of instruments and equipment was used by the band when they played their last ever British concerts at Knebworth, Herts, in August 1979. Details were supplied by Benji Lefevre.

JOHN PAUL JONES:
Keyboards. Yamaha GXl Organ, Yamaha GP 70B electric grand piano, Hohner Clavinet.
Bass pedals. Bill Dunne Custom pedals, Taurus pedals.
Bass guitars. Alembic 4 and 6 string basses.
Keyboard amplification. Mavis 15 x 6 parametric desk, Crown power amps, Showco M4 cabinet.
Bass amplification. GMT 600B amp, and two Carwin Vega cabinets.

JIMMY PAGE:
Guitars. Three Gibson Les Pauls, one Gibson SG double neck, one Gibson RD Artist, one Fender String Bender Telecaster, one Fender Stratocaster, one DanElectro guitar.
Amplication. Two Marshall 100 watt amps, four Marshall 4 x 12 cabinets, MXR phase 90, Cry Baby Wah-Wah, Echoplex, Eventide Clockwork Harmoniser, one Theramin put through a 100 watt Marshall and two Orange 4 x 12 cabinets.

JOHN BONHAM:

Ludwig drum kit comprising 26 inch bass drum (with a spare tuned the same way); 5 inch deep snare drum with 42 strand snares; a 16 x 16 inch top mounted tom tom and 16 and 18 inch deep floor tom toms; and one pedal tympani drum. Paiste cymbals included a pair of 16 inch Sound Edge hi-hats, a 24 inch ride and 16,18,20 and 22 inch crash cymbals. He used a 36 inch paiste gong.

John did not use Syn drums but on his 1976 recording of *Moby Dick* at Montreux, Switzerland, he used Barcus Berry pick-ups taped to all his drum heads. 'We spent three weeks doing it,' says John's old drum road manager Mick Hinton, who kindly supplied the above information.

Drum stage monitor system: Mavis 15 x 6 parametric desk, Crown power amps, two Showco cabinets, two Showco F horn bass bins.

STAGE MONITOR SYSTEM:

Stephenson 30x8 monitor desk, Crown power amps, four Showco M4 cabinets.

PA SYSTEM:

100,000 watts. Showco 30 x 8 superboard, Crown power amps, Roland Space echo, Echoplex, Eventide Clockworks Harmoniser and keyboard unit, two instant phaser units, two digital delay line units.

ONE

GOTTA BE GOOD TONIGHT

'Jimmy – the new album is a masterpiece!' Led Zeppelin's attorney beamed enthusiastically as the huge black limo sped from Kennedy Airport into Manhattan. 'Don't give me that New York bullshit,' returned Jimmy Page, twenty-five-years-old, worldly wise and in the throes of conquering America. The attorney chuckled, unabashed. His sales pitch was dated, but he knew he was right.

It was October 1969 and Led Zeppelin were embarking on their fourth tour of America that year. The first show was due that night at the prestigious Carnegie Hall, scene of much musical history, but which had seen nothing to equal the debut of the blazing hot young British rock band.

These two one-hour shows brought home the depth of emotion that the band's sizzling performances aroused in the hearts of fans. For Americans had taken Led Zeppelin to heart, with their very own brand of unabashed fervour. They hooted, whistled, cheered and reached out to shake hands with the brash heroes from across the Atlantic – Jimmy Page, Robert Plant, John Paul Jones and John Bonham.

The band had been together for barely a year, and had run into a brick wall of indifference when they started out at home. But now British fans, still dazed and confused after the break up of Cream and the virtual disappearance of the Jimi Hendrix Experience, were catching up and turning on. As Zeppelin stormed around the festivals and concert

9

halls of England, so audiences warmed and they too hailed them as idols of the new decade.

From those heady, exciting pioneering days, Led Zeppelin went on to break records, make history and establish themselves as one of the most popular, powerful and successful rock bands of all time. They made fortunes, inspired whole generations of imitators, were honoured by the Government for their services to exports, won endless polls and awards, and became the stuff of legends, myths and fantasies. At their peak they had the world at their feet, with albums turning platinum, gold and silver even before they were released.

Led Zeppelin were four proud and talented men whose career spanned twelve years of hard rock campaigning. To the world they seemed cocky, defiant, protective, overpowering, rumbustuous, outrageous, intimidating. They were also earthy, romantic, eccentric, strong and yet strangely vulnerable. Together with their manager Peter Grant, they were an apparently unassailable team.

To some their very success posed a threat. It made them a target. They aroused envy and jealousy almost from the moment they came into existence. Their greatest strength was their music, and their greatest weakness was the power that riches brought them. Tragedy and folly cast them adrift. In the end, they floated away, deflated, exhausted.

But Led Zeppelin's flight was thrilling for the millions who came along for the ride. Nothing can detract from their achievements and the memory of a band who started out with such hopes and determination. And how they worked. Led Zeppelin were players. They were the ultimate in gigging rock bands. Guitar, bass, drums and vocals and a spot of keyboards. Nothing fancy. There was no philosophy to be espoused, no particular category to stick them in, no labels to be attached.

Those who saw them as just a loud, heavy metal band got it wrong. Those who saw them as mere teenybop sex symbols got it wrong. Just as I got it wrong the first time I saw and heard them, at the Marquee Club in London.

I stared aghast at the figure of Robert Plant, a mass of golden curls, his face and body contorted like a satyr, screaming high notes that threatened to shake even his powerful torso apart. The battering drums of John Bonham broke all bounds of good taste. And what was the quietly-spoken ex-Yardbirds guitarist doing in the midst of all this bombast and mayhem? The somewhat precious and insular English rock cognoscenti of the day were shocked and alarmed by the spectacle.

Yet for anyone who went beyond immediate impressions by listening to their first album, everything began to take shape and make sense. Something startling was afoot, a great upsurge of vigour and determination, irresistible even among the most conservative and reaction-

10

ary. *Led Zeppelin* truly was a masterpiece. It was done in a rush – thirty studio hours – and yet made most previous rock albums sound weak and ineffectual. The production ensured that the band's sound was not just captured but distilled and supercharged. The guitars, drums and organ, not to mention Robert's sensuous harmonica, roared with a blues power that ran rings around the efforts of many a worthy R&B group. Even today Zeppelin's first album has yet to be surpassed for its electrifying atmosphere, spontaneity, ideas, mystical sound quality and 'live in the studio' excitement.

From the first few bars, the album defined Zeppelin's approach and music and signalled due warning of more to come. It boasted a pantheon of block busters. *Good Times Bad Times, Babe I'm Gonna Leave You, You Shook Me, Dazed And Confused, Your Time Is Gonna Come, Black Mountain Side, Communication Breakdown, I Can't Quit You Baby* and *How Many More Times.*

It was a tour de force that served to introduce the talents of Robert Plant and John Bonham, emphasised the organising skills and musicianship of John Paul Jones and finally unveiled the full extent of Jimmy Page's guitar wizardry.

They had good reason to be proud and excited as Atlantic Records unleashed the album and watched its mercurial progress up the charts over the ensuing months. For Jimmy Page it represented freedom after many years helping others to success. Some were quick to describe the album as 'eclectic' and delighted in claiming this and that riff had been borrowed. In fact blues man Willie Dixon was given full credit for the theme of *I Can't Quit You Baby* and *You Shook Me*, and if some other blues and folk themes had been borrowed and re-worked then it wasn't exactly the first time this had happened in the history of popular music.

Led Zeppelin steam-rollered the opposition, seduced doubters and welcomed legions of dedicated admirers. Yet Zeppelin were for many years an underground band in the Sixties sense. They refused to appear on TV pop shows. They wouldn't release singles and ran their operations in a curiously makeshift way. They sneered at the idea of plush offices, and throughout their career only kept up dusty, sparsely furnished chambers. They set up their own record label, Swansong, but the very title, like the name of the band, had a kind of fatalism about it, as if they expected to have to cut and run. It was a joke of course. Led Zeppelin were never in danger of being a flop from first to last. For years they knew only cheers and accolade, but they never quite lost the wariness of self made men. They demanded loyalty and were dismayed by criticism.

But then the rock business had for years been a hotbed of intrigue where innocent young musicians were stitched up by promoters, worked to death by managers and usually left penniless and broken hearted when the lure of pop success was replaced by the realities of failure. It was not even deliberate exploitation in many cases. The lambs were led willingly to the slaughter. The so-called music industry itself lacked experience and professionalism. But things were changing. Zeppelin wouldn't be part of some misguided record company marketing strategy. Their ideas were their own, and when they weren't they borrowed them with style.

Their self-contained air disconcerted many, but the result was success without danger of artistic compromise. Zeppelin were determined to avoid the mistakes of Cream, The Experience or Blind Faith and the benefits of a tight ship operation were obvious.

Such matters were of little concern to the fans who were dazzled by the band's impact. The group professed disappointment with the reaction when they first played around the small clubs that comprised the backbone of the British scene. But there was an excuse. Down South at least, Plant and Bonham were unknown Midlanders, the public had never heard of John Paul Jones and Jimmy Page had barely been seen in Britain for months. Clubgoers were confronted with unfamiliar faces and material. Loyalty to older groups made them suspicious of newcomers. They were unlikely to launch into paroxysms of enthusiasm. There had been virtually no radio play and only a few newspaper articles to introduce the band. It was ironic that in the wake of their later success 'hype' was one of the charges levelled against them.

But Zeppelin were never keen on pop style promotion. They took music journalists on tour with them, attended poll awards ceremonies, (showing more grace than many a lesser star), and their record company took out full page ads. But they were as happy with cheap looking fly posters or releasing an eagerly awaited new album in a brown paper bag. If there was one thing Led Zeppelin couldn't stand it was bull. With the strength of their imposing manager around them, they took on petty officials, rip-off artists or anybody looking for a bit of aggro with an even handed firmness. Would-be bootleggers found the tapes torn from their machines if Peter Grant caught them in the act. Sellers of bootleg material had their premises raided. As far as Peter, the one-time wrestler, actor and tour manager was concerned, Zeppelin were his family, and while they weren't exactly mollycoddled, nobody was going to push them around while he was there.

Once Zeppelin were passing through an American airport where a ship's company of sailors in uniform were in the transit lounge. The sight of the English boys in their long hair, and in particular Mr Page in his always imaginative clothing, aroused hostile jeers and badinage. Peter came from behind, lifted one impertinent tar off his feet and suspended him aloft with a menacing cry of 'What's your problem Popeye?'

Despite all their efforts, there was a flourishing trade in illegal bootleg albums and even a steady business in autographs. Robert Plant frequently fell victim to apparently genuine fans asking for signatures, which he supplied with charm and consideration, until it was noticed that the same men were following around to get as many as possible, for re-sale at exorbitant prices.

If Peter and the Zeppelin entourage sometimes took what seemed like drastic action, it was born out of outrage. There were many who came to fear and resent this hard line and much of the rumour-mongering about Zeppelin over the years came from those who felt they had been ill-served or bore some grudge. Letters were written to music newspapers alleging that the band were about to split up which in turn fuelled more potentially damaging rumours around the world. The band read such stories about themselves with stony indifference.

It was the unprecedented speed of their success in the hugely competitive climate of the early Seventies which caused most behind the scenes jealousy and upset. The rock scene was enjoying unprecedented growth. After the Beatles years it was half expected that the boom was over. Instead the hunger for rock grew.

Where once there had been a few bands touring small clubs and gigging at exclusive discos, now there were myriad bands performing at vast outdoor festivals, in sports stadiums and arenas. From a few English pubs, the music spread right round the world, exciting fanatical followings in Europe, America, Australia and the Far East and inspiring the birth of rock scenes in all these far flung outposts. Within a few years came the concept of the Super Group and the platinum album. Right at the forefront of this outburst of activity were Led Zeppelin.

They were the first band to show that a musical event could be a two or even a three hour concert, and not just a forty minute filler squashed between a variety of acts on a package tour. They showed what could be done with a proper rock concert.

Nowadays when every band plays at the Hammersmith Odeon at least once in its brief life, and cannot conceive going out without a truck load of gear and sophisticated lighting, it is perhaps hard for people to visualise what the rock business consisted of before the advent of Zeppelin, Pink Floyd, Yes and all the rest who set such high standards. The Rolling Stones and The Beatles had made the concept of pop groups familiar to everyone, and part of the fabric of life, like washing powder and holidays abroad. But however famous the group, the hardware was still primitive and the circumstances surrounding a gig singularly unsophisticated.

Bands like The Shadows or The Tornados, were expected to use the theatre's PA system, single microphones and a couple of footlights if they were lucky and the doorman let them backstage. There was no miking of drum kits, and as the music got louder and wilder, so the results were more of a shambles, with equipment breaking down under the strain.

Bass drum pedals snapped, cymbals cracked, amplifiers blew up and the sound balance was usually atrocious. I can remember going to the Woolwich Granada to see a rock package show starring Little Eva (who had a hit with *Locomotion*) where all that could be heard was the tenor sax player screaming and honking.

To be fair Cliff Richard and The Shadows were among the first to obtain a good clean 'live' sound, but even into the age of The Jimi Hendrix Experience, The Who and Cream, amateurism in the sound department reigned. It didn't matter so much when, for example, The Cream played in the Klooks Kleek, West Hampstead, a tiny packed room where you could hear the sound of the drums, bass and guitar in close proximity. And bands like R&B favourites, Georgie Fame & The Blue Flames and Zoot Money's Big Roll Band, relied on the inner balances inherited from the modern jazz era. As soon as the venues grew larger and the power levels went up, there was trouble.

Roadies learned to become sound technicians and musicians learned to be showmen, but it was a hard struggle. The Rolling Stones' concerts were often an embarrassment once they had shed their protective army of screaming teenyboppers and wanted to be taken seriously. Even shows by The Who and Jimi Hendrix' Experience could seem anti-climactic and desultory, and Cream too often relied on long in-strumental jams to carry them through.

What Zeppelin did was to learn how to pace a show, mixing up blues, ballads and rockers, slotting in acoustic sets and building towards a climax in a way which previously had been only dimly understood. Often for the Sixties groups, this simply wasn't possible. I can recall a show that featured Traffic, The Who, The Herd and Tomorrow. Nobody played for more than about twenty minutes to half an hour, and while it was fun, it wasn't practical.

Other bands were attempting to improve the status of the concert and their own sound, like Yes, who experimented with PA systems, at one stage buying up a whole bunch of domestic hi-fi amplifiers in the vain hope this would bring new perfection. The answer lay in the bass bins, huge speakers of a type discovered by Iron Butterfly in old cinemas.

Soon the recalcitrant jobsworths were being shown the door, and theatres were taken over by the groups on arrival. They insisted on the right amount of time to set up increasingly sophisticated equipment, with masses of speaker cabinets, amplifiers, mixing desks, stage moni-toring, and miles of cable. Complete light shows were transported along with the sound gear. Zeppelin eventually brought the new advanced technology of laser beams into play, as well as huge 'live action' projection screens.

Led Zeppelin tried harder in every department and by the Seventies, had perfected the art of the rock show. Other bands scaled more extravagant heights. But it was Zeppelin who lifted rock by the scruff of the neck and turned it from a youth club pastime into big league stuff.

They evolved quite quickly from their power-packed but relatively short club sets to concert marathons. And they were far from being over-slick or too polished. They too ran into dull patches. But however many times the band played their most famous numbers, there was rarely a poor or failed concert. There were erratic moments, like the occasion when John Bonham was late on stage during a concert in Japan. He turned up for his solo *Moby Dick* sounding ill and irascible, as can be heard on the bootleg album *A Cellarful Of Noise* on Flied Lice Records.

On what is a most revealing and rather sad insight into the strain of heavy touring, Robert Plant can be heard plaintively calling for 'Bonzo . . . Mr. Bonham'. The audience start a slow handclap and an anguished Robert sympathises and says 'I know what you mean,' while Jimmy takes the opportunity to tune up his guitar and makes no audible comment. It is left to Robert, the man with the microphone to organise a chant for 'Mr. Bonham!' When there is still no sign he mutters 'F*** you mate' and launches into a spun-out version of *Tangerine*, after observing that perhaps Mr. Bonham had gone for a bath with a Geisha girl.

Cheers greet his arrival at the end of the song, and Robert says concernedly 'Where were you man? We were all shouting for you. It's been like Workers' Playtime up here.' Bonham croaks confused and breathless 'What are you doing – *Tangerine*?' He batters briefly at his snare drum, then groans 'I don't wanna play.'

Robert is having none of it. He announces loudly. 'On drums. . . . ' Bonham snaps back 'Max Wall'. The sudden use of the name of a famed English comedian does not deter Robert. 'Max Wall', he cries. Defeated, Bonzo gets down to work but adds one last defiant cry of 'Ugly I am!' before launching into a slow, but heavy work out in waltz time.

This interlude casts unwelcome light onto the realities of touring, and the kind of stress that could affect the most together of bands. Clearly the nightly cocktail of high living and hard playing took its toll on the health and nerves of the sturdiest. Ill and unhappy, Bonham summoned inner strength and eventually played a most extraordinary solo with his bare hands, a routine which frequently drew blood. He even played his 'Max Wall' march. Humour was never far absent, even in Bonzo's darkest hours.

Not surprising then that Zeppelin should be so against illegal pirate recording, not so much because of the episode of the missing drummer but because of the poor sound quality they presented. It had taken

15

technicians years to cope with the huge output and range a rock band produces. Zeppelin's technical standards were of the highest and Jimmy Page especially hated anything that was second rate.

They were loud but never loud enough to be painful; there was always a dynamic, human quality about their music. They set out to involve audiences and didn't just bash them over the head with incessant riffs. Apart from their most basic compositions, like *Communication Breakdown*, Zeppelin rarely relied on simple repeated figures, preferring to develop themes and interweaving patterns. They reflected Jimmy's own guitar style which among all the great rock guitarists, has been the least definable.

The interplay between Robert and Jimmy was another important early feature of Zeppelin music. In essence it was the 'call and response' idea that had developed in the blues and could be traced back to ring shouts and field hollers – the encouraging whoops that helped black slaves cope with toil in the cotton fields. It was the same theme that permeated gospel music, and was a key factor in swing, as developed by the composer Fletcher Henderson. His 1930s arrangements featured trumpets answering saxophones in whole sections, on such tunes as *Down South Camp Meeting*.

Both Page and Plant were genuinely fond of the blues and well informed about its heritage. Their understanding and natural exuberance ensured that when Jimmy's guitar howled and Robert screamed back, the boys from suburbia captured the positive charge of such ethnic interplay, and transmitted it to audiences who could be wound up to fever pitch, just as swing fans had been wound up by frenzied jitterbugging and killer diller riffs.

Led Zeppelin created blues music of their time, meeting the needs of modern audiences responding to their own tastes and musical upbringing. They represented the state of the art.

The British, ever the happy amateurs, had taken up the sport of reviving American music many years before Zeppelin. It had been an approved activity to form traditional jazz bands, rediscover the lost arts of skiffle and the blues and rescue folk music of all nations from oblivion. It was a practice akin to restoring old steam engines. And unfortunately some of these bands sounded more like slow moving freight trains than sleek expresses. But all this ground work, including the science of discography, helped pave the way for the entire British contribution to rock. The pioneer enthusiasts recovered lost 78 rpm discs from the priceless American archives, and introduced whole new generations to the ferment of jazz and the poignancy of the blues.

Rock and roll created a vast audience for exciting music but it was skiffle, revived by Chris Barber and Lonnie Donegan, which opened the floodgates of home brewed talent. The simplicity of the music meant school kids could have a go at making noises of ther own and not just rely on buying their weekly supply of records.

Cheap guitars, washboards, kazoos and tea chest basses supplied the means, Practically all the famous names of British rock started in this way, the most notable example being The Beatles. The guitar became the nation's favourite plaything. Skiffle replaced roller skates and stamp collecting. As kids taught themselves to play, they progressed to electric amplified guitar and drums. They practised until their fingers were raw. By the Sixties some were ready to make music their careers and there was what became known as 'The Big Beat Boom'. Quite a few booms came and went before Led Zeppelin finally exploded onto the scene in a fireball of energy and experience.

Led Zeppelin had many advantages over the pioneers. They were no studious revivalists, debating the finer points of their cultural heritage. They simply played, with all the power and know-how at their command. They were also young and goodlooking enough to be shot to a level of stardom and achievement beyond the wildest dreams of the schoolboy skifflers and art school buffs of a decade before.

Yet in a sense Led Zeppelin had taken a step backwards. Rock in the Seventies had begun to experiment with electronics and the classics. Zeppelin restored the bulwark of the blues.

Many have sought explanations for their success and appeal. There was no magic formula. They simply did it all so much better than the rest, and they did it together, as a team. The quality of their sound alone made them so much more effective than bands who had dominated rock right up to Zeppelin's emergence. Jimmy Page's production methods made heavy use of echo and he ensured that the bass drum and bass guitar wear given due prominence. This formed a solid platform for the hysterical, almost girlish screams from both vocalist and guitarist. Strong sexual overtones and Robert Plant's ambivalent appeal to both male and female fans was not lost on audiences or critics. Usually white imitators had emasculated Black American music. Zeppelin projected sex appeal even though Robert, the chief protagonist, professed to find the whole thing a joke. It wasn't funny to those American writers in sex and fan magazines who waxed lyrical about his golden hair and bare chest. His tight blue jeans exuded an eroticism which manufacturers of heavy duty industrial wear might have found surprising.

Fan magazines the world over sported full colour glossy pictures of Robert whenever they wanted an eye catching cover shot. Thus Plant was enshrined in a number of famous poses, hugging, nay embracing himself, stroking, pouting, groaning, gasping for air, in all shades of ecstasy en route to an orgasm. Clad in a variety of blouses, usually floral in design, with a bondage necklace, dripping with rings and wristbands, Robert easily outshone Rod Stewart, Mick Jagger and all the

17

other sons of the footlights.

Sometimes he wore white satin pants, but invariably reverted to his old blue jeans, heavy with bulges, belts and golden zippers. His camping was delivered with a blend of self-mockery and engaging innocence. But his hand on hip impudence sometimes made it difficult for him to control unruly crowds who wanted to let off fire crackers and whistle when he wanted them to be quiet. Then he was the school captain, trying to quell the mob. Off stage people were in awe of him, overwhelmed by his exhuberance and flashing humour, until he put them at rest with smiles and consideration. The British affected not to notice Robert's universal charms. Americans had no such qualms. In teenybop magazines they raved over his sex appeal. One writer proclaimed: 'Robert has been responsible for some of the most exciting, sexy vocals ever heard on record . . . he can do a slow moody song and have us all wishing we could get closer and help him not be so blue.

'And Robert has got to be one of the sexiest dressers in rock. His outfits can really fire up the imagination, especially those shirts which never seem to have buttons on them...' Teens Now, April 1975).

Jimmy Page too was considered to have his own brand of sex appeal. With his violin bow flashing about the place and curly black hair cascading over his eyes he was dubbed both 'secretive and romantic'. He too was not above baring his chest in the cause of rock 'n' roll and wore satin pants with the best of 'em. But Jimmy, who could look positively dashing in a suit, was also prone to let a straggly black beard besmirch his face, and strolled around in the most sartorially offensive collections. Hideous tartan trousers, shapeless overcoats and idiotic hats all combined to disfigure Jimmy and reduce him to the level of an impoverished down-and-out, instead of projecting himself as a handsome rich pop star. Doubtless this was his perverse intention.

Of the rest of the band, John Bonham in his early years had stolid good looks and unlike Jimmy looked most impressive in a beard. His warm expansive smile signalled peace messages when his personal storms had passed. John Paul Jones bore a mysterious air of inner turmoil. How any of this breed of eccentrics and ego maniacs ever put up with each other for a minute remains a mystery.

But it seemed to work. There were brotherly bonds that refused to be broken, no matter how many times it was alleged in the press that the band was on the verge of splitting up. Certainly those bonds were put to the test for many a gruelling year.

From the moment Led Zeppelin went gold and the band played their first US concerts (supporting the MC5 and Vanilla Fudge), there began a non-stop saga of artistic and statistical triumph. Recording and touring kept them under public scrutiny virtually throughout the Seventies. The only breaks came when they were physically disabled by accidents

18

and disasters.

It was no wonder the band developed a reputation for causing mayhem on the road. There were plenty of groups, British and American, who indulged in such pranks as smashing up dressing rooms and hotels, which seemed like prison cells as the endless tours blurred into a dream – or nightmare. Zeppelin sometimes played six nights a week for a month without a break. They did six sell out tours of the States in one fifteen month stretch. Still the world clamoured for a visit. And so they went – to Japan, Ireland, Italy, Germany, anywhere the fans were eagerly waiting.

Sometimes there were riots. In Milan 15,000 fans and police fought a pitched battle. When they played in Perth, Australia, they drew five per cent of the entire population. When they toured England every ticket for every show was sold out within hours of box-offices opening.

In 1973 they broke a record for the 'largest audience attendance' when 56,000 came to see them in Tampa, Florida. That one show grossed over three hundred thousand dollars. In 1977 they broke their own attendance record, when more than 76,000 went to see one show at the Silverdrome, Pontiac, Michigan on April 30.

There was hardly any time for the individual members to indulge in the favourite extra-curricular activity of supergroups – solo projects. When they weren't touring or resting at their palatial country residences, the band were rehearsing for new albums. After the first two seminal albums there was immense pressure on them to go on producing follow-ups to Whole Lotta Love, which had been a smash hit in America in 1970. It is to the eternal credit of the band that they didn't take the easy route. They experimented, explored and produced albums that didn't always gain immediate understanding and acceptance. In fits and starts came Led Zeppelin III and IV followed by Houses Of The Holy, Physical Graffiti, and towards the end of their career Presence, The Song Remains The Same and In Through The Out Door.

Zeppelin songs seemed to gain life and meaning by repeated plays and often the most stony material proved rewarding on closer examination. There were times when their writing got stuck into brick wall situations where the creative juices wouldn't flow. And then came the surge of relief when a song or a theme just took off, and ascended to the heights. One of their most celebrated songs was Stairway To Heaven which appeared on the untitled album which became known as The Four Symbols, Zoso, Led Zeppelin IV or The Runes Album. For an untitled album it sure had a lot of titles.

Stairway To Heaven became an FM radio favourite in America where it was played almost as many times as Layla by Eric Clapton. It was a perfect melody, sung with restraint by Robert, and with a feeling for the lyrics which he usually managed to summon, however many times he

19

was called upon to sing it. It was another example of Led Zeppelin evading categorisation. And when, in the mid-Seventies, they looked to be sagging, they returned with the immensely powerful and action packed double LP *Physical Graffiti*. This yielded *Trampled Underfoot*, a piece of pure funk that astonished fans when they played it at five shows at London's Earls Court Arena. Another new Zeppelin anthem, *Kashmir*, ran for nine minutes and impressed even the new breed of rock cynics eager to debunk the established stars. The rising tension and drama of this piece was probably one of the band's most original compositions, an Eastern Jewel In The Crown of Zeppelin's Empire.

Even though the band were often tempted to escape from the demands of the public and the strictures of those who would be their judges, they did feel a responsibility towards the huge and eager audience they had created. There were only a few periods when there was no new album on stream, with 1974 being recognised as one year when the band went to ground, and 1977 the year when tragedy threatened to put an end to all further activity.

They held parties, attended galas, gave charity shows, revisited old haunts like the Marquee, and even made a movie, *The Song Remains The Same*, which some dubbed a 'home movie' unaware of the Video Age just around the corner.

Then came the accidents, traumas . . . and deaths. Some called it karma.

There was no doubt bad luck dogged them. But examined rationally, it was only the result of the risks anybody runs when they lead an active, pressurised existence. The sheer number of miles travelled meant that statistically the members of Led Zeppelin stood more chance of running into trouble than those who stay home and watch TV. And so Robert narrowly missed being crushed by his car when it fell off its jacks. Then he was injured in a car crash in Greece in 1975, which confined him to a wheelchair for months. And Jimmy Page crushed a vital finger in a train door at the start of a major American tour.

There was worse to come. In 1977, Zeppelin's black year, four members of the Zeppelin entourage were involved in a fight with the staff employed by US promoter Bill Graham, arrested and charged with assault. Just three days later, on July 26, Robert Plant heard that his five-old-year-son, Karac, had died as the result of a mystery virus infection. Robert returned immediately to England.

After a long period of rest and recuperation, during which many rumours suggested the band would split up, the group went to Sweden in early 1979 to record their new album – which would prove to be their last studio production – *In Through The Out Door*. They had already assembled the previous May for a month of rehearsals at Clearwell Castle in the Forest Of Dean, and Robert had returned to singing with unpublicised jam sessions in England and Ibiza.

The new album was pure Zeppelin with no discernible influences from the changed pop scene. Songs like *In The Evening* had a romantic sense of nostalgia. It would prove to be Zeppelin's real life swan song.

They played two concerts at Knebworth on August 4 and 11, 1979, their first in Europe since 1975 and their first U.K. dates since the Earls Court shows of 1975. By August *In Through The Out Door* was Number One album in charts around the world.

In 1980 Zeppelin began a full European tour which began on June 17 in Germany. The band were in high spirits and played well. One night their old mate, drummer Simon Kirke from Bad Company sat in and jammed alongside Bonzo. They were having such a good time they decided to tour America once more – in the autumn – now that the nasty business of their punch up a few years before had been settled.

But before they could set off, tragedy struck again. John Bonham was found dead at Jimmy Page's Windsor home on September 25. He was discovered by John Paul Jones and, at the inquest held in October, it was stated that Bonham had died as a result of a drinking spree.

For a few weeks it was believed that the band might carry on with a new drummer, just as The Who had taken on Kenny Jones when Keith Moon died. But no sooner had one newspaper carried stories of Bonham's replacement, than the band hurriedly announced that they would definitely break up. They could not carry on without their old friend. The song had ended.

At times during its career Led Zeppelin had resembled a juggernaut. Now it lay bruised and battered. 'What was Led Zeppelin's place in rock history?' The best answer is that they created a large chunk of it. Maybe the magic and inspiration had begun to fade even before the end came. Certainly there were many prepared to write them off. They could not have gone on much longer touring with *Whole Lotta Love* and *Stairway To Heaven*. But there was a hint of a new dawn in those last days before Bonham died. There was the extraordinary last cut on their last album *In Through The Out Door* called *I'm Gonna Crawl*. It was a masterpiece. Now we'll never know what might have been. We can only look back at what was.

21

TWO

—

YOUR
TIME
IS
GONNA
COME

—

Led Zeppelin, like Minerva, sprang up with a tremendous battle cry, fully armed from the head of the gods. Minerva was the patroness of the arts and trades as well as being something of a warrior. And so it appeared that Zeppelin were fully equipped to take on the world within an instant of their creation.

Most bands who achieved fame in the golden years of rock served long and often dismal apprenticeships. Theirs was the inevitable saga of schoolfriends and classmates, working their way up through youth clubs until they could headline at the Dunstable Civic and gross sixty pounds for their pains. Not so Zep. When they were signed by Jerry Wexler, vice president of Atlantic Records, it was for the sum of two hundred thousand dollars, the highest advance paid to a rock band thus far.

The company proudly announced, in late 1968: 'Atlantic Records has signed the hot new English group, Led Zeppelin, to a long term, exclusive contract. Although the exact terms of the deal are secret, it can be disclosed it is one of the most substantial deals Atlantic has ever made. Agreement for the group's services was made between Jerry Wexler and Peter Grant.'

All of which came as a great surprise to those back home, who barely knew of the band's existence. According to legend, Led Zeppelin 'began in a small, stuffy rehearsal hall in London in late 1968.'

From there it was but a step away from the release of their debut album in January 1969 which went gold as it topped the charts. Atlantic were delighted they had taken heed of the words of singer Dusty Springfield. She had recommended the band simply because she knew the work of arranger John Paul Jones. Although Atlantic had been eager to sign a British group, they were in need of assurances. After all, the band were already insisting on complete control over production and merchandising, and nobody from the record company had even seen them perform. It all confirmed their godlike status and conferred on Mr Grant the sort of management kudos previously attained by Brian Epstein.

Zeppelin seemed the archetypal overnight pop sensation. Yet they had roots deep in the motherlode. They came together virtually as strangers, but they had a shared experience and common aims. The key factor was timing, and Jimmy Page had got it just right.

Jimmy had that inner determination often noted in people who are burdened with illness; glandular fever and a weak disposition made him the last person to embark on a life of constant travelling. But the demands of his chosen career fed him with energy, and Peter Grant was his bulwark in the rock music battle ground. Ultimately, it was Page's driving ambition and frustration that made Zeppelin happen. But for these factors, his undoubted musicianship might have remained hidden, appreciated only by a coterie of fellow players. He certainly served a long and honourable apprenticeship. Said John Paul Jones: 'I rated Jimmy Page for years and years. We both came from South London and even in 1962 I can remember people saying "You've got to go and listen to Neil Christian and the Crusaders - they've got this unbelievable young guitarist." I'd heard of Pagey before I'd heard of Clapton or Beck'.

Pagey was born James Patrick Page on January 9, 1944 in Heston, Middlesex. When fourteen he was given a guitar by his parents and for some weeks took little interest in learning how to play it. Then he heard rock 'n' roll and in particular an Elvis Presley record, *Baby Let's Play House*. He loved the sound of Scotty Moore's guitar, featured on most of the early Presley records. Said Jimmy: 'I wanted to know what it was all about. A guy at school showed me a few chords and I just went on from there.'

The early rock records all had a simple, direct sound, with the guitars, drums and bass cutting through. They had 'presence'. 'They generated so much energy I had to be a part of it. That's when I started.' He also fell in love with folk music and the work of guitar virtuoso Bert Jansch, who Jimmy described as 'a real dream weaver and incredibly original'.

There was little likelihood of Jimmy settling down to a routine job. The nearest he came to such a fate was to go for an interview, while still at school, for a job as a lab assistant. He also considered a career as a

23

painter and went to art school in Croydon. But the lure of the guitar remained strong.

Jimmy never had any formal lessons and said: 'I just picked it up. When I was at school I had my guitar confiscated every day. They handed it back to me each afternoon at four o'clock.' He taught himself by copying note for note the solos he heard on records. Rather than plod studiously through chord books and simple tunes he was aiming at the top.

After leaving school early Jimmy joined his first important band, Neil Christian and The Crusaders, at the age of fifteen. As soon as he had mastered his first chords he had felt the need to play with other musicians, but found this difficult. 'I used to play in many groups . . . anyone who could get a gig together really,' he recalled. 'It was Neil Christian who saw me playing in a local hall and suggested I play in his band.'

It was his first taste of professionalism and life on the road. He had to travel up from Heston to the West End of London, clutching his guitar case and feeling important. Quite early on he was earning good money – twenty pounds a week – when the average wage was only half that.

Most of Jimmy's money was spent on buying better guitars and equipment. He carried around a Gretsch Country Gentleman guitar which impressed local musicians, including Jeff Beck who said: 'It looked huge on him because he was such a shrimp. All you saw was a huge guitar being thrown around by a man who was as thin as a pipe cleaner.'

Jeff Beck, Eric Clapton and Jimmy Page swiftly formed a mutual admiration society. They all played a lot around the Richmond and Eel Pie Island area and each developed his own approach to blues and rock. Jimmy became particular friends with Clapton and always gave credit to Eric for developing the sound associated with the Gibson Les Paul and Marshall amps. The careers of all three men would intertwine throughout the Sixties.

Jimmy's dexterity quickly impressed musicians who saw him with the Crusaders. But few pop fans understood what Jimmy was doing on the guitar in their eagerness to hear cover versions of the latest chart hits. The Crusaders were a cut above most bands and featured a lot of R&B material by Chuck Berry and Bo Diddley which Jimmy loved. But the gruelling life of one-night stands was beginning to affect his health. He suffered from travel sickness and caught glandular fever. Recalled Jimmy: 'We were driving around the country, sleeping in the van and breaking down on the M1. Eventually it knocks you out. I just collapsed from exhaustion.

'After only a few months with the band, I wondered if I could carry on much longer. I was doing a lot of painting in my free time and thought I would go to art college where a lot of my friends had gone.'

He went to college at the age of seventeen to study painting by day and jam at blues clubs by night. 'When I first started at art college, the music scene was pretty depressing. Nobody was interested in Chuck Berry or Bo Diddley. All people wanted was Top Twenty stuff and trad jazz. Then about a year later everything started to happen. The Stones broke through and there were the Liverpool and R&B scenes coming together. I enjoyed playing again and R&B restored my faith in pop music. But I really wanted to be a fine art painter. I was sincere in that aim and when I went to college I kept quiet that I played guitar or else they would expect me to play in the lunch hour. A conflict arose between music and art and it came to the point where I had to make a decision. I had to leave because I couldn't do both.'

Jimmy played with the Cyril Davies All-Stars at the Marquee. Davies was a fine harmonica player who died in January 1964. He was one of the key figures who introduced Rhythm & Blues to England, starting out as a banjo player in trad jazz and skiffle bands. He helped form Blues Incorporated with Alexis Korner and left to form his own band based on the Chicago blues of Muddy Waters, a style then totally unknown to British audiences. Among his sidemen were Nicky Hopkins, the piano player, and singer Long John Baldry.

Page gained invaluable blues experience from these jams but, ironically, his presence at the Marquee led to a complete change of course. Instead of working his way up through a succession of groups, as did his partners Beck and Clapton, Jimmy became a session man.

Now there was a way he could take part in the booming pop scene, without going on endless one-nighters. Said Jimmy: 'I used to jam with a group at the old Marquee when Cyril Davies was still alive. One day someone asked me if I wanted to play on a rock session – and that's how I started.' The request came from producer Mike Leander and it led to Jimmy becoming the first of a new breed of young session players. He played on literally hundreds of record dates between 1963 and 1966. He lent his exciting, powerful guitar sound to many a big name band who couldn't get their act together in the studio. He bolstered those groups who had more fame than talent and eventually produced many singles himself.

He played with a huge variety of professional musicians, string and brass players who sometimes mocked his loud guitar work. When he let off steam after a session with some blazing chords, they would stick their fingers in their ears, insulating themselves from the sound of the future.

He gained insight into the workings of the studios and their equipment and learnt the art of production. Jimmy was much in demand. Producers were crying out for the 'modern sound' that their regular men couldn't deliver. Page proved both young, adaptable and reliable. Much

25

to Page's surprise and alarm he found himself featured in an article about his work in the Sunday Times colour magazine. He had become a star of the Swinging Sixties.

Despite this publicity, it still came as a surprise in later years when it was realised that Jimmy had been responsible for so many distinctive riffs on records by Them and a dozen others. He even worked on famous hit singles by The Kinks and The Who. Jimmy thought it most 'uncool' to go around loudly proclaiming his role but there were times when he felt it reasonable to put the record straight and he talked to me about his session career.

He explained: 'Everyone likes to play around with different people and it can be stimulating to do sessions with other groups. But the kind of work I was doing became completely stifling. Never being involved with the artist it was like being a computer. When I started, only Big Jim Sullivan was around and if there were three sessions he could only do one and the others would end up with . . . well no names mentioned! Without Jim they were desperate. From then on, work for me escalated. I had a crash course in session work. There was no individuality involved. The arranger said: "This is what you play," and that's what I played. I got fed up. It became a pain in the neck. When the Yardbirds came up . . . that was it.'

Jimmy's first session was *Diamonds*, a 1963 hit featuring Jet Harris and Tony Meehan, ex-Shadows who had formed a successful duo. Next he played on *Momma's Out Of Touch* by Carter Lewis and the Southerners. Said Jimmy: 'They were both hits and that gave me the impetus to keep on doing it.' Jimmy's role was to strengthen weak links. He was the producer's insurance policy to prevent time-wasting. Sometimes there would be three guitarists on a session, including the supposed star. The guitar sound was in vogue, but later on, producers started going for strings, brass and keyboards. The Stax riffing style also meant there was less opportunity for a creative solo; Jimmy got into a routine that became a rut. Sometimes 'fixers' booked him for sessions without telling him what the music was going to be, and he'd find himself making 'Muzak' to be piped into supermarkets.

Despite his protestations that he grew bored with the scene, there were many sessions he enjoyed and where he did feel involved. He worked as house producer and arranger for the new Immediate label, one of the first 'independents' run by Rolling Stones' manager Andrew Loog Oldham. He produced albums and singles for Twice As Much, Chris Farlowe, Fleur De Lys, Nico and John Mayall and the Bluesbreakers. With Mayall he produced *I'm Your Witchdoctor* and *Telephone Blues* which featured Eric Clapton on guitar. Jimmy also recorded some blues sessions with Eric which were later released by Immediate, on the LPs *Blues Anytime Vol. 1 & 2*.

26

This historic association began when Jimmy and Jeff Beck went to see Clapton play at a gig with the Bluesbreakers. Eric came and stayed at Page's home for the night and in the morning they got up and started jamming on guitars with a two-channel Simon tape recorder running. When Jimmy was producing the *Telephone Blues* session with Mayall, he mentioned he had the early morning jam tapes with Eric to Immediate. The record company claimed possession as Page was under contract. They wanted to release them, even though they consisted of one long jam. Several of the tracks were outtakes of one number.

Page was unhappy they should be released, but insisted that at least the tapes be cleaned up. Mick Jagger overdubbed some harmonica, while Eric was promised royalties. 'Eric and I got split writing on the tunes but I don't remember getting any money out of it, I don't know if Eric did,' he said later. 'It was a bit of a drag that those should ever have come out. I just had no power at all to stop them.' It was another lesson about the music business that served Page in good stead when he was calling the shots.

During the peak of his session period he found himself working with The Pretty Things, The Rolling Stones, Jeff Beck, Donovan, Georgie Fame, Herman's Hermits, and pop artists, Petula Clark, Val Doonican, P. J. Proby, The Bachelors, Dave Berry and the Cruisers, Crispian St. Peters, Lulu, Burt Bacharach, Jackie DeShannon, Marianne Faithfull and Tom Jones. He was on Tom's 1965 smash *It's Not Unusual*.

One of his finest and most memorable contributions was his work on Joe Cocker's *With A Little Help From My Friends* in 1968. The distinctive, haunting guitar intro impressed itself on the collective memory of a generation. The performance was notable for the use of church organ and pregnant silence in the opening bars before Joe's plaintive vocal begins. It was an idea which would be fully expanded on *Your time Is Gonna Come* on the first Zeppelin album, cut later that year.

Jimmy played on The Who's *I Can't Explain*, their first hit in 1965. Said Jimmy: 'Actually I wasn't really needed, but I was fortunate enough to find myself there. Just strengthening the riffs, that's all – just two guitars doing it, instead of one.' Jimmy played a couple of phrases on the B side as well, called *Bald Headed Woman*. He contributed more to sessions by Them with ill-tempered Irish singer Van Morrison. It was Jimmy's guitar which created such atmospheric excitement on *Baby Please Don't Go*, *Gloria*, and *Here Comes The Night*.

Page talked to Dave Schulps of Trouser Press magazine about the Them session. 'It was very embarrassing because you noticed that as each number passed, another member of the band would be substituted for by a session musician. It was really horrifying. Talk about daggers! God, it was awful. There would be times you didn't want to be there. The group went in thinking they were going to record and all of a

27

sudden they found these other people playing on their records.'

Jimmy also experienced tension when he was called in by producer Shel Talmy to help out The Kinks. He played on The Kinks' first album *You Really Got Me*, but the band didn't really want him around. There had been a great deal of fuss in the newspapers about session men playing on pop stars' records, and the band didn't want to be involved.

Jimmy bumped into a huge cross section of artists on his treks around the studios and not all were taciturn and resentful. He met singer Jackie DeShannon and they formed a songwriting partnership. Soon Jimmy was getting royalty cheques for songs he'd written for Marianne Faithfull, P. J. Proby and Esther Phillips. He was perhaps regarded as their key to the nether world of rock.

He got on well with his fellow session men and in particular drummer Bobbie Graham, who recorded a version of the old Louis Bellson drummer's favourite *Skin Deep*. Jimmy co-wrote the B side *Zoom, Widge And Wag* and played on both. It featured lots of echo on the drums and the bass drum in particular was given great prominence, a voice screamed 'Wow' in unison with the drums and Jimmy soloed with the rather strangled tones and jerky phrasing typical of the times. The era of more relaxed and sustained notes was still some way off, but this 1965 opus gave some hint of the kind of heavy rock that lay in the future.

Jimmy sounded very enthusiastic on this project which is perhaps more than can be said for a hilarious solo he contributed to a track on an LP by the Irish singers, The Bachelors, hugely popular in the Sixties. They made a Decca album called *Bachelors' Girls* in 1966 and for once Jimmy was given, not just a credit, but an honourable mention in dispatches. A quite dreadful song called *Lovely Kravezit* provided Jimmy with a chance to take a few bars. Explained the sleeve notes: 'She is the swinging crazy chick in a bevy of beauties. She affected us all very much, particularly Jimmy Page and his guitar solo.' This was played completely out of tune accompanied by a lugubrious tuba. It was the kind of sound parodied by The Bonzo Dog Doo Dah Band on their classic *Canyons Of Your Mind*.

The work kept pouring in. He worked with Mickie Most, when he was making his own pop singles in 1964 and appeared on *The Feminine Look*, *Money Honey*, and *That's Alright*. Their paths would cross again when Most gave up singing and became a producer.

The Everly Brothers recorded an LP *Two Yanks In England* which utilized Jimmy's services, and another American involvement was when he produced The McCoy's *Hang On Sloopy*, released in Britain on Immediate.

Jimmy even cut his own single *She Just Satisfies* coupled with *Keep Movin'*. It was released on Fontana in 1965 and had a strong Kinks influence. The B side was more of an instrumental rave up, with shouts

28

of encouragement from Jackie DeShannon. Said Jimmy: 'I just did it because I thought it would be fun. I played all the instruments except drums which were played by Bobbie Graham. The other side was the same story. There's nothing much to be said for that record, except it was tongue-in-cheek. I sang on it too, which is quite unique. When I got in the studio I didn't know what the hell I was gonna do. The A side was tongue-in-cheek Kinks. Jackie DeShannon helped me salvage the whole thing. The end product I suppose was a trip to the States to see her. But the record is best forgotten.'

But it wasn't forgotten by discographers. The A and B side of his long neglected solo single turned up on a fascinating album *James Patrick Page Session Man*, issued by the so-called Led Zeppelin Fan Club of Manchester in 1979. The album gives a wonderful insight into the way Jimmy's style developed and the uncredited sleeve note writer points out: 'On this extraordinary handful of obscure 45s we can hear Page mapping out unknown territory, with his use of distortion, speed, feedback and other forms of experimentation that were completely unknown and unrecognised at the time.'

One of my own favourite British beat records of the early Sixties was the version of Chuck Berry's *Memphis Tennessee* by Dave Berry and the Cruisers. I played it endlessly on jukeboxes and it was many years before I discovered that the driving guitar which gave it such an authentic sound was played by Mr Page. Thanks to diligent collectors we were also reminded of his work on less well known rockers, like *Talking About You* by The Redcaps, which was released on Decca in 1963. Sometimes the young Page played a shade faster than his fingers would allow but he always made the most of his brief solo spaces and urged the band on with solid rock riffs, as revealed on the Zephyrs' *I Can Tell*, released on Columbia in 1964.

One of his best early solos was on Dave Berry's *My Baby Left Me*, actually on the B side of the 1964 *Memphis Tennessee*. Often he was just called on to provide extra power as on *I Can't Explain*. But his contribution to *Baby Please Don't Go* by Them, released the same year, was amazing. It made the record as much as Van Morrison's vocals, with echoing, dramatic sustained notes and flurries taken at a gallop. His answering phrases and carefully placed licks on *Here Comes The Night* was another sound that roared anonymously round the world.

And so the work went on, as Jimmy played on countless jingles, film scores, commercials; so many that even he cannot remember them all. Sessions where he had control stood out, like Fifth Avenue's *The Bells Of Rhymney*, a B side which he wrote, produced and arranged. John Paul Jones was the bass player on the session.

In 1965 Jimmy was asked by the Yardbirds' manager, Giorgio Gomelsky to replace Eric Clapton who had quit the group, but Jimmy turned the offer down as he wanted to stay on the session scene and didn't think he was ready for another dose of touring. Jimmy recommended a fellow guitarist who had played on the same circuit with him around Richmond and Eel Pie Island, Jeff Beck, who was then leading The Tridents. Jeff took the job and later invited Page to join him in the Yardbirds. But for a while longer Jimmy held out. He had his job as house producer for Immediate Records, where he backed Chris Farlowe on *Out Of Time* and on some demos made by Mick Jagger and Andrew Oldham. But the ration of short breaks on B sides was beginning to induce feelings of extreme frustration, especially as so many of his friends were going on to freedom and stardom, like Eric Clapton in Cream. In 1966 Jimmy finally accepted Beck's invitation to join The Yardbirds.

The opportunity came when Paul Samwell-Smith, the bass player, decided to leave after Keith Relf, their singer, became somewhat tired and emotional at a concert in Oxford. Jimmy volunteered to help out until they found a replacement bassist. After a while Chris Dreja switched from rhythm guitar to bass and Jimmy played dual lead guitar with Beck. The session years were over.

Jimmy recalled his return to singing. 'When The Yardbirds came up – that was it. I was a good friend of Jeff Beck who had replaced Eric Clapton. I was there when Paul Samwell-Smith had a great row and left the group, so I had to take over on bass. I had never played one before. Then Chris Dreja swopped from rhythm guitar to bass and the idea was for me and Jeff to get a stereo guitar sound. With two lead guitars it worked really well. Lots of people have done it since, but I think we must have been the first.

'When we went over to the States we took them by storm. The funny thing was the Yardbirds didn't mean anything as a group in England. There was no magic attached to the name. In America it was different. Hollywood went wild. Anyway – it was an exciting group.'

British reviews were very cool about the new line-up as Jimmy recalled: '"The Yardbirds appeared with their cacophony of sound." That's what an English paper said when they reviewed a show we did at the Albert Hall. But in those days groups used the Albert Hall PA system and you know what that's like. The guitars were really loud – and bad! Eric had always used a little amp and that was Keith Relf's big complaint about Jeff and me. "Eric used to play through an AC30 and you've got 300 watts each!" He got more and more reticent, but nobody was trying to drown him out. Obviously there was a lot of tension and that's why he made two solo records.'

The Yardbirds were one of the best loved and most popular of the early British R&B groups. They had sprung to fame in the Richmond area after they replaced The Rolling Stones as resident local group, and

30

had a succession of hit singles including *For Your Love* and *Shapes Of Things*. The original line-up included Eric Clapton, Paul Samwell-Smith, Keith Relf, Chris Dreja and Jim McCarty. The Yardbirds became famous as a breeding ground for guitar talent, even though as a band intent on recording songs and experimenting with production ideas, they didn't always make the best use of their talents. They had also had endless management and contractual problems and felt they had got little in terms of financial rewards for their efforts. If Jimmy had seen how records should and shouldn't be made from his years in the studios, he now had a lesson in the pitfalls of group management. He also saw how internal squabbles could wreck a band.

The bust up which led to Paul Samwell-Smith resigning came when Keith Relf embarked on a heavy drinking bout at the Oxford May Ball of 1966. Upset at the indifference to their music shown by the upper class crowd, he began insulting the audience, blowing raspberries at them and rolling around on the stage for a whole number. The band had to drag him off stage and play twenty minutes of instrumentals.

Keith was taken home where he fell down stairs. Later he discovered he had broken all the fingers in his hands from trying to break some plastic trays with mock karate attacks. It was all a disaster and Samwell-Smith was furious. When he stalked out, the band lost their producer and the man responsible for much of their new found musical direction, as well as a bass player. Fortunately, Keith's disgrace and Paul's fury didn't deter the man who would replace him, and who just happened to be in the audience watching the scene with great amusement.

Chris Dreja would recall the arrival of Page in his book Yardbirds (Sidgwick and Jackson). 'Jimmy had obviously had enough of doing sessions and wanted to tour and play in front of an audience. He seemed very easy going and was always smiling, but there was a lot going on behind that; he was a very shrewd guy. When it became obvious that it was going to be permanent, he was very happy to stay and although it wasn't his normal instrument, he was happy to remain on bass. He just liked being in the band.'

As soon as he joined, the band were off to America and Jimmy had his first taste of Stateside touring, in a hired DC3 airliner. When the band played at the Carousel Ballroom, in San Francisco, Jeff Beck collapsed and Chris switched to bass while Jimmy played lead. It was like a practice run for when Beck would leave, which they expected at any-time. When Jeff came back to the group, Jimmy stayed on lead. They began sporting the 'dual lead, stereo sound' which was featured on their recording *Happenings Ten Years Time Ago*. It wasn't a hit but it established the sound which would provide a basis for rock for the next decade. Said Jim McCarty, the drummer: 'It was too advanced for its time, which is why it wasn't a bigger hit.'

Jimmy's arrival had helped Jeff get out of a rut, but Beck continued to behave in unpredictable fashion, generally being late, not turning up until the end of a session and causing upset in the ranks. Poor wages and hard touring were blamed for Beck's intransigence. In the end the rest of the band wanted Jeff out and Jimmy couldn't say anything that would change their minds. But before Beck left, the two guitarists recorded a cut called *Psycho Daisies*, the B side of *Happenings*, and they also collaborated on the soundtrack to the Antonioni film *Blow Up*. The director originally wanted Pete Townshend to appear and smash his guitar up. The Who wouldn't do it, so the Yardbirds got the part and Jeff Beck was asked to smash a guitar – a fake one – instead. This cameo role at least captured the band and the crazed atmosphere of the Sixties – on film. The band's tune for the film was called *Stroll On*.

More tours followed including a package with the Rolling Stones and Ike and Tina Turner, which was one of the few occasions when British fans got to see Beck and Page together. I recall seeing them at the Marquee, but it was all a bit of a shambles.

Jimmy looked smart with a bouffant hair style, sideboards and satin, sequinned jacket. He had the quiet smile of someone who knew that at least he was getting his act together when all around him were falling apart. One problem was that Jeff couldn't handle the competition and would try to blow Jimmy off stage. Page was always on the ball, but Jeff's returning fire in guitar exchanges would be unpredictable and relied on volume when accuracy failed. As Chris Dreja recalled: 'When it worked, it was incredible, all those stereo riffs and alternating voices, but it frequently degenerated into a wall of noise.'

In October 1966, the Yardbirds returned to America for a four week stint on the Dick Clark Caravan Of Stars. The band were billed alongside pop acts and they were badly treated by bullying tour managers. They had no sleep and hated every minute. Jeff Beck did one show then walked off the tour. He was supposed to be ill and wanted to be with his girlfriend in the Californian sunshine, not spend his time cooped up on a bus. You couldn't blame him in that respect, but the band had to fire Jeff and Jimmy told them he could carry on with the tour. After all – they had a contract to fulfil. There was a business meeting and afterwards Jeff asked Jimmy if he was quitting too. 'No, I'm going to stay. I want to try and work it out.' But he had a hard task ahead of him.

Said Jimmy: 'It got to the point where Relf and McCarty couldn't take it anymore. They wanted to go and do something totally different. When it came to the final split it was a question of begging them to keep it together, but they didn't. They just wanted to try something new.' Jimmy had been delighted at getting out of the session scene and desperately wanted his first major group to be a success. They hadn't even recorded a proper album. There was still work to be had but recalled Jimmy: 'Keith in particular would not take gigs very seriously; getting drunk and singing in the wrong places. It was a real shame.'

During the tour the Yardbirds decided they needed a manager, a new one, and they were introduced to Peter Grant. He had enormous experience in the music business and a forceful personality. If anyone could save the Yardbirds it was Grant. He took the band off to Australia and Singapore on a package tour with Roy Orbison and the Walker Brothers. Much to the Yardbirds' amazement, the tour was a success.

Jimmy was much impressed by their new manager's capabilities. He had known Peter since the days when he worked at Immediate Records. Their office was next door to record producer Mickie Most's set up and Peter and Mickie worked together. On the return to England it was decided to put the band's recording career into the hands of Mickie, who had been responsible for many hits by the Animals, Herman, Donovan and the Nashville Teens. Mickie, who had been a singer in the Most Brothers, was one of the brightest talents on the scene and seemed to have a Midas touch. He even managed to help Jeff Beck get a hit single with *Hi Ho Silver Lining*. Later, in 1969 he formed his own independent Rak label which produced a stream of hit artists. But he was not so successful with the Yardbirds.

The group had liked his work on the Donovan records, but somehow the combination just didn't work out. They recorded *Little Games*, an album released in America on the Epic label in 1967. Some of the tracks were good, but the track *Little Games* was quite awful with trite, flower power dippy lyrics. Even Jimmy's spirited guitar work couldn't save it. There were items of interest that pointed to the way ahead. Jimmy used the violin bow on his guitar for the first time on *Tinker, Tailor, Soldier, Sailor* and was featured on a showcase number *White Summer*.

Out in the field, Peter Grant took the Yardbirds by the scruff of their unwilling necks and took them on tours of France, Belguim, Germany and Sweden. For the first time in their careers, they made money from gigging. But there was the age old problem of 'musical differences'. Keith and Jim were heavily influenced by the acid rock scene. They wanted to be groovy while Page wanted to get into hard electric rock.

In the spring of 1968 the band was booked for their last ever American tour and played at universities and ballrooms. Unluckily the worst gig on the tour turned out to be at the Anderson Theatre in New York, the very place chosen for a 'live' album. Said Jim McCarty: 'The Anderson was a horrible place, cold and unfriendly.' But Epic went ahead with plans to record and set up a few microphones. 'Pathetic' thought the group when they saw the engineer had put only one mike over the drum kit.

Jimmy Page's monitor speaker was miked up instead of his proper guitar amplifier and as a result they lost all the fuzz and sustained guitar

33

notes. Although the band played well it was realised that a so-called 'live' album would sound terribly lame, so cheers, allegedly from a bullfight, were dubbed on! The album *Live Yardbirds With Jimmy Page* (US Epic E30615) was not released until 1971. Jimmy immediately had an injunction put on the record and caused it to be withdrawn. It reappeared again briefly in 1975 and was later circulated as a bootleg. It gave a fascinating insight, for all its flaws, into the way the Yardbirds were going and how their music was well on the way to becoming Zeppelin music. But the Yardbirds no longer had the heart to keep up the pace. They had cult status in America but were virtually forgotten at home. Their disappearance was regarded as a mystery after all the excitement they had created only a couple of years before. All around there were new groups forming, better equipped to cope with rock's new demands.

The Yardbirds split up after returning to England in the summer of 1968. Their last gig was performed at Luton Technical College in July. Jimmy immediately began laying plans for his own group. Chris Dreja, rhythm guitarist turned bass player was more interested in photography now than music, but toyed with the idea of joining Jimmy's New Yardbirds. His enthusiasm evaporated after one rehearsal. The founding members of the old group drifted off, away from the mainstream of events. Keith Relf, their frail, blond haired singer and harmonica player, who suffered from a collapsed lung and had bravely battled his way into the British R&B scene with such enthusiasm, and later became so disillusioned, died in tragic circumstances. He was electrocuted by his own guitar, while practising at home in 1976.

During the period when Beck and Page worked together Jimmy wrote and produced a tune called *Beck's Bolero* which appeared on the B side of *Hi Ho Silver Lining*. The line up was star studded ... Beck and Page on guitars, Nicky Hopkins (piano), John Paul Jones (bass) and Keith Moon (drums). It gave Jimmy the idea of forming a group with himself, Beck, Moon and Nicky Hopkins. Instead of having John Paul Jones on bass, Keith Moon suggested bringing in his old friend John Entwistle on bass and vocals.

After much discussion they decided to a have another singer instead. Their first choice was Stevie Winwood, but he was too involved with his own band Traffic, and it was felt he wouldn't be interested. Their next thought was Steve Marriott of the Small Faces, one of the best singers in British rock. He was approached and recalled Jimmy: 'He seemed full of glee about it. A message came through from the business side of Marriott which said: "How would you like to play guitar with broken fingers? You will be if you don't stay away from Stevie." After that the idea just sort of fell apart. Instead of being more positive about it and looking for another singer, we just let it slip. Then The Who began a tour

34

and The Yardbirds began a tour and that was it.'

One of the great 'What Ifs' of history faded away but at least it left a legacy in terms of a name for the group. Discussing their chances Keith Moon had pronounced that the band would go down 'like a lead balloon.' John Entwistle agreed – more like a Lead Zeppelin.

In the wake of the Yardbirds debacle Jimmy began looking around for musicians to join him. Jimmy was working on the session which produced Donovan's hit *Hurdy Gurdy Man* and John Paul Jones was the arranger. During a break he asked Jimmy if he could join his new group on bass. There were still some Yardbirds dates that hadn't been fulfilled and Jimmy planned to call his band The New Yardbirds. He was helped by Peter Grant who was to be manager of the new band, and ex-Yardbirds roadie, Richard Cole.

Jimmy's first choice for a singer was Terry Reid who could also play second guitar. But he had just signed to Mickie Most as a solo artist. Terry suggested they try out an eighteen-year-old Midlands singer Robert Plant. Jimmy and Peter went to see the unknown vocalist performing with a band called Hobbstweedle at a teachers training college, in Birmingham. Jimmy found Robert singing to an audience of about twelve people with most of the students in the bar drinking. But he thought Robert was fantastic. 'Having heard him that night and having listened to a demo he'd given me of songs he'd recorded with The Band Of Joy, I realised his voice had an exceptional and very distinctive quality.'

Robert came to Jimmy's house at Pangbourne and they discussed musical plans. Jimmy was capable of playing in so many different styles he wasn't quite clear in his mind which direction to pursue. But the power of Robert's voice made him realise that hard rock was the only way to make full use of all their pent up energy.

They had guitar, vocals and bass and keyboards. Now they needed a drummer. They desperately wanted someone who would be a good time keeper and could rock with unflagging energy. Robert immediately recommended his old friend John Bonham who had played with him in The Band Of Joy. But Bonham was now working with American singer Tim Rose and earning what he thought was good money in a steady gig.

Robert went to Oxford to catch up with Bonham and took him to one side at a gig to say 'Look mate you've got to join The Yardbirds.' John's reply was 'I'm alright here aren't I?' But it wasn't the money that finally made him join the band. He knew the kind of music Robert played and respected Page and the legend of the Yardbirds. He made his decision and went to the first rehearsal. It was held in a small, stuffy room in London in September 1968. Said Jimmy: 'The four of us got together in this two by two room and started playing. Then we knew – we started laughing at each other. Maybe it was from relief, or maybe from the knowledge we could groove together. But that was it. That was just how well it was going.'

Then came the matter of a name for the band. They could call themselves The New Yardbirds as long as they were playing the old band's remaining dates. They considered calling themselves The Mad Dogs, until they remembered the name that John Entwistle and Keith Moon had suggested on the *Beck's Bolero* session. Said Jimmy: 'The name was not really as important as whether or not the music was going to be accepted. We could have called ourselves The Vegetables or The Potatoes. I was quite keen about Led Zeppelin. .... '

Led Zeppelin's launch into the crowded skies of rock was about to commence. They had lift off!

THREE

A WHOLE LOTTA LOVE

Sixties guitar heroes came with a package of personality problems. They were invariably hung up, frustrated, incoherent and ridden with adolescent angst. Jimmy Page had none of these failings. He was sharp, shrewd and filled with a great sense of fun. Jimmy was always laughing, joking and was particularly amused by the antics of his fellow musicians. A dazzling smile and friendly manner quickly disarmed new acquaintances, while a steadiness of character inspired trust and confidence.

Jimmy in his twenties was a slight figure, good looking, almost feminine, with a soft musical voice and gentle manners. Long black, curling hair, a penchant for mismatching clothes and artistic tastes gave him the air of a nineteenth century aesthete. One could imagine him as part of Oscar Wilde's circle, a painter with entrée to the houses of the rich and famous. But giggles and secretive glances over the shoulder concealed a tougher inner man.

He disliked incompetence and unprofessionalism. He resented any attempts at manipulation. One of the reasons why he first refused an offer to join the Yardbirds to replace Eric Clapton was because he didn't like the way the offer was put to him. The manager told him that Clapton was taking a holiday. Jimmy didn't want Eric to feel he had come in behind his back.

Jimmy talked in a wonderfully quaint form of Home Counties English. Yet this rendered any riposte, or snapped retort all the more telling. He swore when he felt the need for emphasis but never adopted any American mannerisms despite all his years touring the States, not to mention his incarceration in recording studios where most slang is of U.S. origin.

Instead his friends and associates were 'chaps', anything that gained his approval was 'jolly good' and before retiring to bed he would drink a 'night cap' or a 'hot toddy'.

Many were astonished such a mild mannered youth could assemble and guide the fortunes of a band that would become a byword for uproar and bombast. Odder still that he should be surrounded by a cast of characters who could have starred in a Hollywood epic about invading barbarian hordes. But Page was not alone. He had help from another remarkable man who loomed large in his affairs.

Peter Grant had begun managing the Yardbirds in 1966. Both in appearance and personality Page and Grant seemed poles apart, which perhaps explains why they got on so well. There was a deep bond of friendship and affection between them, a kind of silent alliance that did not need to be demonstrated in loud chatter. They drew strength from the partnership and influenced each other in matters of taste and art. They were interested in art, books and antiques and together they would go on buying expeditions.

The close relationship between group and manager was much envied by other bands. They would have loved to have the same kind of manager who could obviously weave business miracles and still relate to his boys like an omnipotent father figure. One such group, Emerson, Lake and Palmer hoped that Grant would take them over, but he was only interested in one band.

Peter, born in 1935, had worked his way up through British showbusiness the hard way. A wartime evacuee, his education had been disjointed when he left school at thirteen to become a stage hand at the Empire Theatre in Croydon. He tried manual work in a sheet metal factory, but knew that life had to offer something more exciting. He worked as a messenger in Fleet Street, delivering pictures for Reuters until he was called up into the Army for National Service. He attained the rank of corporal. It was all good training for running a pop group. Back in civilian life after two years he worked a holiday camp for a season, and then at a hotel in Jersey.

Back in London he worked at the legendary 2Is Coffee Bar in Soho where so many stars of skiffle and rock 'n' roll had been discovered, including Tommy Steele. Peter was employed as a bouncer on the door and met another wandering soul lured by rock, Mickie Most, who was working there as a waiter. They were paid ten shillings each for their services.

Peter needed more than ten bob a week to live on. He took up wrestling for over a year, and then took the next logical step. He became an actor.

Sometimes Peter 'doubled' for the well known thespian Robert Morley, and was also offered small parts in a TV series with Tony Hancock, and in BBC TV's famed *Dixon Of Dock Green* police saga. One of the biggest box-office movies he appeared in was *The Guns Of Navarone*. But after a while he grew tired of film work which required early starts and lots of hanging around doing nothing. The call of rock was still strong, and he was asked to act as tour manager for visiting American stars being promoted in Britain by Don Arden. Among them were Gene Vincent, Little Richard, and Jerry Lee Lewis. Having coped with that lot, taking over the management of the Alan Price Combo seemed a lot easier. After a succession of decidedly odd jobs Peter had now found his true vocation. The Combo later became The Animals, managed by Chas Chandler and produced by Peter's old mate, Mickie Most. Both men were coming up fast.

When Peter went to America with the Animals and later the Yardbirds he could see that the days of the hit single were over as far as the long term career of bands was concerned. The underground rock scene was breaking and it was more important to get into the new venues the movement was spawning. He got the Yardbirds booked to play at the Fillmore, San Francisco run by promoter Bill Graham and they were the first British outfit to play there.

Peter did his best for the Yardbirds but could see their problems. He recognized that Jimmy Page was easily the most outstanding member and grew to admire and respect his talent and attitude. Said Peter in an interview: 'I felt I was closer to Jimmy than any of the other members. I had immense faith in his talent and abilities.' If Jimmy wanted to go it alone, then Peter would be ready to back him up. 'I just wanted him to do whatever he felt was best for him at that time,' said Peter. When the group Jimmy wanted was finally assembled, Peter was all geared up to take the music business by storm. It was a source of chagrin when the business didn't immediately recognise their talent.

Said Peter: 'I had been going to the States since 1964 when I went with The Animals. I learned a lot while I was there. By the time I got Zeppelin I knew American inside out. Before we got the (first) LP we couldn't get work in Britain.

'It seemed to be a laugh to people that we were getting the group together.' Peter resented the attitude that he was wasting his time when as far as he was concerned, Led Zeppelin was a matter of the utmost importance. He would have liked to pick up the entire business by its ears and give it a good shake.

The harsh fact was that in London, both Plant and Bonham were

39

unknown Midlanders, while even Jimmy had not been seen in action beyond a few under publicised Yardbirds gigs. He was respected, something of a legend among fans, but the vast mass of the music orientated public were unfamiliar with either the faces or the material. The old Yardbirds were regarded as a spent force and nobody was about to exhibit paroxysms of enthusiasm about 'The New Yardbirds'.

My first inkling of the dawning of a new era came when Jimmy Page walked (as I recall) unannounced into the offices of the Melody Maker, then in Fleet Street. I felt strangely honoured that this underground hero should have sought me out, and it turned out there was a connection. I had not long since interviewed Neil Christian of Crusaders fame and Jimmy had noted my references to his old friend and boss. Jimmy was very keen to give the first details of his new band. It was around October 1968 and the headline on the subsequent article ran 'Only Jimmy Left To Form New Yardbirds'. There was something about Jimmy's enthusiasm that made me feel he was on the brink of something exceptional although I hadn't the faintest idea that Zeppelin would be such a powerful beast. The Yardbirds with Eric and later Jeff had been one of my favourite bands. I was just pleased they were coming back.

Thus, in the preface to the interview I wrote: 'Whatever happened to the Yardbirds? One of the great mysteries of our time, ranking with the Devil's Footprints and the Marie Celeste is the disappearance of a group once hailed as the most progressive in Britain.' After a brief history of the band I introduced Mr. Page. 'Well spoken, good looking and good natured, he was once one of Britain's youngest session guitarists, his ability to read and feel modern pop making him much in demand. He gave up the security of the studios to hit the road and play his own solos.'

Jimmy explained what happened to his previous group: 'We didn't do any gigs in England for two years, so no wonder we lost popularity. But just before we split we did a couple of colleges that were really fantastic. I was knocked out. We were a happy group and used to get on well socially until we got on stage and Keith lost all enthusiasm. I used to say "Come on, let's make an effort," but it had all gone. When they split I think it did us all a favour because the new chaps are only aged nineteen and are full of enthusiasm. It was getting a bit of a trial in the old group.'

My article continued: 'The line up of Jimmy's new band (and he's not sure whether to call them Yardbirds or not), includes John Paul Jones, Robert Plant and John Bonham. They made their debut in Denmark.'

I had just missed their secret debut by a couple of days. I had been at the Tivoli Gardens in Stockholm on tour with The Marmalade, and had been puzzled by posters proclaiming the imminent arrival of 'The

40

Yardbirds' a group which by then seemed defunct.

Now Jimmy could explain all, while I kicked myself for having missed this bit of history making. 'The music is blues basically, but not Fleetwood Mac style. I hate that phrase 'progressive blues'. It sounds like a hype, but it's more or less what the Yardbirds were playing at the end, but nobody knew about it because they never saw us. We're starting work on an LP and we're going to the States in early November. I'm hoping the Marquee will be a good scene. Robert can get up and sing against anybody. He gets up and sings against Terry Reid! Those two are like brothers together.

'I thought I'd never get a band together. I've always shied off leadership in the past because of all that ego thing. I know old Eric wanted to get a thing together with Stevie but neither of them likes leading. I didn't *want* The Yardbirds to break up, but in the end it was too much of a headache. I just wanted to play guitar basically, but Keith always had this thing of being overshadowed by Jeff and that, which was nonsense. It was great fun when we had the two lead guitars.'

Jimmy talked about the future: 'It's refreshing to know that today you can go out and form a group to play the music you like and people will listen. It's what musicians have been waiting for for twenty years.' The New Yardbirds played ten dates in Sweden before making their British debut at Surrey University on October 15, 1968. They played the Marquee Club on October 18. The event was advertised as 'The British Debut of The Yardbirds' and they were supported by a band called Sleepy. Next they played Liverpool University on October 19 and from then on changed the name to Led Zeppelin. There was still some confusion over the spelling and 'Lead' was used until 'Led' settled the correct pronunciation.

One of the first critics to see the band in action was Tony Wilson of Melody Maker. He was impressed but had a few reservations. Nonetheless, he predicted they would become one of the biggest names of 1969 and added 'they will do well in the States'. He went to see them at the Marquee and wrote: 'Led Zeppelin the re-grouped Yardbirds made their Marquee debut last week. They are now very much a heavy music group with singer Robert Plant leading and ably holding his own against a powerful backing trio. Amp troubles didn't help them but there seemed to be a tendency for too much volume which inevitably defeats musical definition. One of the best numbers of the set was *Days Of Confusion* (sic) featuring interesting interplay between Plant's voice and Page's guitar on which he used a violin bow creating an unusual effect. Drummer Bonham is forceful, perhaps too much so, and generally there appears to be a need for Led Zeppelin to cut down on volume a bit.'

Tony had started out as the Melody Maker's folk correspondent so his

41

chaffing at the volume was understandable. He was actually much more enthusiastic about the band than his review would have us believe and was particularly excited about the singer. I remember him bringing the first copy of the Zeppelin album into the office and us standing about shaking our heads in disbelief at the sound of screaming long drawn out howls echoing even above the scratch and rumble of the Melody Maker's primitive record playing apparatus.

The group returned to the Marquee on December 10, this time billed as Led Zeppelin (née The Yardbirds) and were supported by the Bakerloo Blues Line. It was apparent that the band was a sensation. Page had found a superstar in Robert Plant, whose power and vocal range was simply stunning. There had been good singers before on the Marquee's sweat and beer soaked stand – Stevie Winwood, Roger Daltrey, Jimi Hendrix – but none of them could match Robert's sonic attack. His whoops and roars interwined with Jimmy's liberated guitar, heard in its full glory for the first time.

The new star vocalist seemed cocksure, sexually precocious and full of boundless energy. He got off on the excitement the band was generating and seemed to be heading for a state of nirvana that everyone in the audience was welcome to join, once they had cast aside inhibitions. At first the reticent English could only stand and stare.

Blues fans were a rather serious lot in the late Sixties, and as I went to see Zep at the Marquee and such venues as Cooks Ferry Inn in North London, it was obvious that they didn't quite know how to handle the brash newcomers. They were used to mumbled words, and long, slow, guitar solos. Zeppelin seemed intent on starting a four man riot.

But Robert should have been used to the club scene. He'd been a stalwart of the Birmingham scene for years. He was born Robert Anthony Plant on August 20, 1948 in Bromwich, Staffordshire. His father was a civil engineer and Robert had a career mapped out for him, as a chartered accountant.

As a kid he picked up any instrument that promised a quick route to rhythm and tune and so he learnt to play the harmonica, kazoo and washboards around the time of the skiffle boom. He soon progressed to the blues and was always much more impressed by Black American artists than the somewhat lame white British rock 'n' rollers of the period.

His interest in the blues was aroused while at school by a friend called Terry Foster, who he later discovered had been involved in the Yardbirds, before Keith Relf joined them. Robert's early groups all featured deep country blues music and the works of Memphis Minnie, Bukka White and Skip James. Robert told me about his early days in an interview during the mid-Seventies: 'To start at the beginning I had been surrounded by English rock way back in the early Sixties. Some of it was very ballsy, but the majority of it was half-baked, and didn't seem to be coming from any place in particular. I'd listen to say, The Fenmen when they came to the town hall, but I didn't know that *Money* was a Barrett Strong thing. You always heard these things in the context of English rock. Then I'd start to find the originals on the London-American label and a lot of obscure labels that they didn't even know much about in America. But stuff from Chris Kenner on the Minit label was coming out of New Orleans. The pop music in America was coming direct from local roots. I started going back to listen to Snooks Eaglin and then I heard Robert Johnson for the first time when I was fifteen.

'One of the things I picked up from Robert Johnson when I started singing was the liaison between the guitar playing and his voice. It was so sympathetic it almost seemed as if the guitar was his vocal chords.

'There was a tremendous amount of emotional content in the guitar and the vocals. It was the most amazing thing I'd ever heard. I think Muddy Waters took a lot from his style.'

Robert could express himself through the eternal medium of the blues which gave him freedom to explore and develop his voice and range. He soaked up records by particular favourites like Buddy Guy and Willie Dixon. But he could offer no rational explanation why his voice had such tremendous power. 'The voice really started developing when I was fifteen and I was singing Tommy McLennan numbers', he said in an early Melody Maker interview. 'I don't really know why it's as powerful as it is.'

As a kid Robert was mad about girls, music and football. His tastes haven't changed much over the years. 'I forgot about lessons and kept joining pop groups,' said Robert recalling his schooldays. His friend Terry Foster played eight string guitar in the style of Big Joe Williams and recalled Robert: 'He was a horrible bloke at times but he was a real white bluesman and when I was fifteen I fell immediately under his spell.'

Robert started performing at the Seven Stars Blues Club in Stourbridge where he played harmonica with the Delta Blues Band. Robert's father used to drop him off at the club and then he'd get his rocks off on tunes like *Got My Mojo Working* in the company of local musicians like Chris Wood, later with Traffic, and with guitarist Stan Webb who formed Chicken Shack. Plant was also involved in the more serious folk club circuit although he found the concept of enthusiasts sitting in rows of chairs, silently smoking pipes, stroking beards and mulling over the significance of the lyrics rather unnerving. He soon learned that he needed an audience that responded, and showed signs of life. His father meanwhile still hoped that he would settle down to a proper job and he started training to be a chartered accountant. But after three weeks he fled the course and went back to college to get a few 'O' levels.

43

Recalled Robert: 'It was getting to the stage where I only dared to go home at night because my hair was so long. So at sixteen I left home and started my real education musically ... moving from group to group, furthering my knowledge of the blues.'

His first ever gig was with Andy Long and the Original Jurymen in Leicester. He depped for the lead singer who had got laryngitis. Then came the Delta Blues Band, and the New Memphis Bluesbreakers, which had a floating personnel, depending on who turned up for the gigs. This was the intellectual blues scene Robert found a bit over his head and he went on to join The Black Snake Moaa, a band named after a song by Blind Lemon Jefferson. Joked Robert in an interview with Steve Gett: 'It would be terribly hard to guess what the old black snake was.' Robert played guitar in the group for a while before joining The Banned, which had jazz overtones, and then The Crawling King Snakes. Now the English music scene was being influenced by the first influx of Stax records. Rhythm sections were beefed up. Modern black music became acceptable in the dance halls and discos. It was altogether more fun, funky, hip and groovy. And Robert could groove with the best of 'em. Real, live American artists came to Britain, like Otis Redding, Roy C, Solomon Burke and Wilson Pickett, all greeted as messiahs and usually saddled with duff support groups. But it was an exciting time to be coming up. The clubs were booming and there was a great hunger for live groups, in the age before home taping, sound systems, mobile discos and synthesisers.

Robert loved playing to the crowd, who in their turn, often stopped their chatter and drinking to turn round and watch the wild and hairy singer pouring his heart out. Working equally hard was a ferociously heavy young drummer who had just joined the King Snakes – John Bonham, nicknamed Bonzo. It was the first time Bonham and Plant had met.

Robert's reputation began to grow and he was asked to join The Tennessee Teens, a three piece Tamla influenced band. When Robert came in they changed their name to Listen and in 1966 Plant, aged eighteen, made his first ever recording; a single called *You Better Run* with Listen and two more on his own, *Long Time Coming* and *Our Song* all issued on CBS. Robert enjoyed his time with Listen which went on the road for extensive tours where they bumped into Rod Stewart and The Steampacket with Long John Baldry. The latter could well have influenced Robert's sense of camp humour and stage manner.

The music became a cheerful mixture of Tamla, Mod R&B and Muddy Waters style blues, all of which suited Robert, but eventually there had to be a change. As well as singing, Robert was writing material and needed a band that could use it. He formed the first version of The Band Of Joy but was eventually sacked for telling the drummer he was slowing down. Their manager also claimed that Robert 'couldn't sing'.

The Band Of Joy had been influenced by the West Indian blue beat music popular among Birmingham's immigrant community.

But the next version of The Band Of Joy – Robert used the name for his new group – was influenced by the first manifestation of psychedelia. They had painted faces and wore kaftans, beads and bells. 'It went all right for a while, but we were frightening our audiences to death!' said Robert. Robert drove the van to gigs and brought in his old mate John Bonham on drums. But they could only get two gigs a week. This was the third version of the band, impressed by new bands from the West Coast of America, in particular Moby Grape and Love, featuring Arthur Lee. The Band Of Joy got as far as London on its travels and played at Middle Earth on the same bill as Ten Years After and Fairport Convention. They were earning sixty pounds a night but there weren't enough gigs and Robert's girlfriend, Maureen, kept them afloat with her day job.

Robert had to start labouring to bring in some more money. 'Actually I believed that I would be on the dole. But I wasn't going to give up. For a while I was living off Maureen, God bless her. Then I did some road making to earn some bread. I actually laid half the asphalt on West Bromwich High Street. All it did for me was give me 6/2d per hour, an emergency tax code and big biceps. All the navvies would call me 'the pop singer'. It was really funny.'

Despite all his efforts, Robert couldn't keep The Band Of Joy together much longer. The music scene was now in a state of flux and turmoil and the old blues was giving way to the experimental sounds of Pink Floyd, The Nice and King Crimson. Even Birmingham produced its own sons of psychedelia in Traffic with Stevie Winwood. The Band Of Joy split and John Bonham, who still hadn't recorded with anybody, went off to tour with American singer Tim Rose who came to Britain to work and had a big hit with his slowed down version of *Hey Joe*.

Robert sang for a while with Alexis Korner who always had an eye and ear for new talent, and was then involved with the highly obscure band Hobbstweedle, until he was rescued by Jimmy Page and Peter Grant. 'The Wild Men Of Blues From The Black Country' would soon find wider fame.

Said Robert: 'The Band Of Joy was really a launching pad for my ideas and my theories about music. My manager got me some acetates of unreleased material from the States, things like Buffalo Springfield. That made me realise that crash-bang music, for want of a better word, could be combined with meaningful, beautiful lyrics and it was a big pointer for me. Then everyone began boosting the Cream up as the greatest thing in the world but I couldn't see it. I'd rather listen to the Youngbloods or Poco. Then The Band Of Joy began to crumble up and

45

all my hopes started to vanish. I worked with Alexis Korner occasionally in a band with Steve Miller on piano and had a wonderful time. I respected them very much for their originality. I didn't know that our ideas were on the same lines. Jimmy Page and Peter Grant came to see me in Birmingham when I was with a group and trying to invade Smethwick with the West Coast sound.

'They suggested that I go to Jimmy's house for a few days to see if we got on together and it was fantastic because I rummaged through his record collection and every album I pulled out was something I really dug. I knew then we'd click. Nobody in Britain wanted to know us, but Jimmy told us it'd be different in the States.'

Led Zeppelin instantly restored Robert's sagging confidence. 'The group really woke me up from inertia. Years and years with no success can keep you singing, but it can bring you down an awful lot.'

Jimmy was astounded when he first saw Robert singing. Not so much by his voice as by the neglect that such an obvious talented artist had been made to suffer. 'When I auditioned him and heard him sing, I immediately thought there must be something wrong with him personalitywise or that he had to be impossible to work with, because I just couldn't understand why, after he told me he'd been singing for a few years, he hadn't become a big name yet. I thought Robert was fantastic.'

The first rehearsals with Robert took place in September 1968. He found the whole experience 'incredibly illuminating.' Everybody was asked for their ideas and contributions and each theme was embellished and altered. Although Robert and Bonzo felt a bit like 'green' young recruits compared to the experienced Page and Jones, they were used to jamming and coping with all kinds of different musical situations. There was a great feeling of spontaneity and a vast wealth of pent up ideas and feelings at last being allowed to bubble to the surface. All four shared the feeling they had hidden their collective light under too many bushels for too long.

John Henry Bonham who had to be cajoled into joining the new band had already begun to taste fame through his work with Tim Rose. He had been featured in a powerful solo that more than matched the work of Ginger Baker in Cream. He had toured with Rose in early 1968 and said Jimmy: 'I went to see him and couldn't believe how he was living his music. He was extremely inventive, more so than any other drummer I've heard. He did his drum solo with his hands.'

Bonham was born on May 31, 1948 in Redditch, Worcestershire. His father was a carpenter and had his own building business. John went to Lodge Farm Country Secondary School, and when he left school went into the trade with his father which he enjoyed. He always said that if the drumming business got bad he could always go back to building work. 'But drumming was the only thing I was any good at, and I stuck at it,' said Bonham.

He had first shown an interest in playing at the age of five. He started drumming on a handy bath salts container which had wire on the bottom, and a round coffee tin with wire attached to give a snare drum effect. He was also prone to hit the family pots and pans, so in desperation his mother bought him a snare drum when he was ten. His dad bought John his first full kit at the age of fifteen and a half. 'It was almost prehistoric. Most of it was rust, but I was determined to be a drummer as soon as I left school.'

He joined his first group, Terry Webb and The Spiders when he was sixteen. They wore purple jackets with velvet lapels and were a right bunch of Teds complete with greasy hair and bootlace ties.

After a year with Terry he joined A Way Of Life and at the same time got married, at the age of seventeen to Pat, a girl he met at a dance in Kidderminster. John worked with Nicky James, a local singer with a lot of talent whose fame had spread as far afield as London. John told me: 'I had a group with Nicky, an incredible singer. But we had so much of the equipment on hire purchase, we'd get stopped at night on the way back from a gig and they'd take back all the PA. Nicky had a big following then, and he could sing any style, but he couldn't write his own material.

'We used to have so many clubs we could play around Birmingham in those days. Lots of ballrooms too. I was so keen to play when I quit school I'd have played for nothing. In fact I did for a long time. But my parents stuck by me. No, I never had any drum lessons but I remember Carl Palmer went. He had a lot of lessons. I just played the way I wanted and got blacklisted in Birmingham. "You're too loud!" they used to say. "There's no future in it." Nowadays you can't play loud enough.'

John promised Pat he would give up drumming when they got married. But each night he came home and sat at the drums for a bash. He had to get back into regular playing and joined Steve Brett and The Mavericks. Next came the Crawling King Snakes where he met Robert. Like the singer, he was pretty broke most of the time. He put all the money he earned from his gigs into buying new drums while his parents helped out with life saving loans.

The fate of the four musicians who were to form one of the most successful rock bands of their time was decided by lucky phone calls and chance meetings. In the case of John Paul Jones he was already familiar with the prime mover, Jimmy Page.

John's real name was John Baldwin. He was born in Sidcup, Kent on January 3, 1946. His father was a pianist, arranger and band leader and so had musical roots, unlike Jimmy (whose father was an industrial personnel manager and mother a doctor's secretary). Although often regarded as the quietest and least noticeable member of Zeppelin, his keyboard and bass guitar work, together with his all round musical skills made a large contribution. He taught himself to play piano as a child and switched to the organ. He took lessons and by the age of fourteen was playing in church. Perhaps the bass tones of a powerful organ also encouraged him to take up bass guitar. He made his own ten watt amplifier and used a Dallas Tuxedo bass which enabled him to join local pop groups.

He worked as a backing musician on BBC Radio's Saturday Club show and began to meet influential people within the business. His big break came when he auditioned for the role of bass player with the Jet Harris and Tony Meehan combo. They had a hit with *Diamonds* which coincidentally featured Jimmy playing acoustic in the background. John was booked into the backing group and went on tour. He went on to become a top session man, one of the new breed of young players who could cope with the demands of the hit makers. One of his strangest chores was to overdub backing tracks to records by Alma Cogan, after her death.

Like Jimmy, he released his own solo record, a song called *A Foggy Day In Vietnam*.

He also worked on records by Cliff Richard, Paul and Barry Ryan, Kathy Kirby, Lulu, and Dave Berry. His association with Dusty Springfield began when he played with her at the old Talk Of The Town venue in London. He also arranged some tracks on her LP *Definitely Dusty*. He went on to work as musical director with Micky Most, and collaborated with Andrew Oldham, in the same working environment as Jimmy. He even turned up on two Yardbirds' cuts produced by Most, *Ha, Ha Said The Clown* and *Ten Little Indians*, in 1967. He appeared on sessions with Jeff Beck, including *Love Is Blue* and the LP *Truth*, and with the Rolling Stones on *Their Satanic Majesties Request*. He worked with Donovan and Jimmy on the *Hurdy Gurdy Man* LP and played bass on and arranged *Mellow Yellow* and *Sunshine Superman*. John also played on many of Herman's Hermits hits.

Like Jimmy, he too grew tired of being in the studios all the time and desperately wanted to join a group, even though he had a wife and two children, and would have to go out on the road for long stretches.

It was during the sessions for Donovan's *Hurdy Gurdy Man* that John Paul asked Jimmy if he could use a bass player for his proposed new group. Jimmy was delighted at the chance of having such a gifted musician in the band. Said Jimmy: 'He had proper music training and had quite brilliant ideas.'

Although John Paul Jones (by now committed to using a stage name), had little interest in the blues, he was willing to learn and began to share Robert's enthusiasm. Said John: 'During our first rehearsals, any feeling of competition within the group vanished after one number.' He was

48

quite happy to be in the background, as he couldn't sing, especially with Robert around, and the bass was the kind of static instrument that didn't require too much showmanship to put across. While he was no more animated than John Entwistle in The Who, John Paul thoroughly enjoyed his first experience of 'live' work in some years once Zeppelin hit the road. He told me after their concert at Carnegie Hall: 'You get to the stage where you enjoy playing so much you don't want to come off stage.'

Before work began on their own debut album, the new band recorded tracks with American singer P. J. Proby for an album called *Three Week Hero*. This was released on Liberty (LBL83219) in 1969 and was produced by Steve Rowland. Proby had been a big star just a few years earlier with hits like *Somewhere*, until his trouser tearing stage act ran into trouble with press and various society watch dogs. On a cut called *Jim's Blues* it was possible to hear the nascent Led Zeppelin in action. While Proby showed that not all Americans could sing the blues, the band consisting of Page, Bonham, John Paul Jones and Robert on harmonica, absolutely shook with power and, itching to play, doubled the tempo and virtually blew Proby, struggling to scream a few words, out of the studio. The album, which provides such a fascinating preview of things to come, now sells for thirty pounds a copy.

Sessions for the group's own LP began at Olympic Studios, London on their return from the Scandinavian tour as the New Yardbirds. The record was finished within two and a half weeks of the band getting together for its first brief rehearsals. Only thirty studio hours were required to record the material. The intention was to get a 'live' sound and Jimmy was aided by fellow producer Glyn Johns. Said Jimmy: 'It only took thirty hours because we knew exactly what we were going to do before we went into the studio.'

Maybe another reason for the rush was the amount of session work that Jimmy had to finish off from previous commitments. Hence the P. J. Proby dates and work on Joe Cocker's *With A Little Help From My Friends* and Al Stewart's *Love Chronicles* albums.

Although the first few gigs were overshadowed by the 'ex-Yardbirds' tag, by the time they played at Middle Earth, the London hippies' venue then held at the Roundhouse, Chalk Farm, on November 9, 1968, the band went down a storm and got two standing ovations. The same day Robert married Maureen. 'That was my honeymoon – playing at the Roundhouse,' said Robert. They earned £150 for the gig and Robert agreed that the band had done well. 'Basically Jimmy was the name but at the same time I think people were aware that he wasn't going to put his name to anything that was half-hearted. And in actual fact everybody was received pretty well. The car broke down on the way – not to the church, to the gig!'.

49

Despite the good response from the hippies, who traditionally kept an open mind about anything new, Peter Grant wasn't pleased with England. He had his eyes firmly on America, where he thought the band would get a lot more reaction than a couple of encores. Jimmy wasn't enthralled by the home scene either. He recalled: 'It was just a joke in England. We really had a bad time. They just wouldn't accept anything new. It had to be The New Yardbirds, not Led Zeppelin. We were given a chance in America. We just wanted to come over to America and play our music.'

Said Peter: 'Zeppelin started in the States on Boxing Day 1968. Three of the group had never been to America before and didn't know what to expect. They did a week with the Vanilla Fudge. My instructions were to go over there and really blast them out. Make each performance something everybody remembered. They really did that.'

As soon as word filtered back to England that Zeppelin had taken off with fans and promoters, there were feelings akin to remorse. Why had they gone to the States to make their name? Said Jimmy, in an interview with Hugh Nolan: 'I knew you could sit around as a new group for months in England and have no notice taken of you at all. For one thing there's very few places to play, and it's pretty unlikely you're going to get any radio plays. In the States a new group can get so much more exposure.'

American critics raved about the band with New York writer June Harris proclaiming: 'Zeppelin are the new Cream! The biggest happening of the 1969 heavy rock scene is Jimmy Page's Led Zeppelin! The reaction to the group's first tour here, currently in process, had not only been incredible, it's been nothing short of sensational.'

There was to be no shortage of sensations for the next twelve years.

FOUR

AMERICAN DREAMS

America loved Zeppelin. They didn't care what was past or future. They were only interested in the present and accepted the band as it existed on face value. They enveloped them with an enthusiasm that was overwhelming. The fans whooped and screamed and yelled. It justified the faith shown by Atlantic Records. There was some upset among executives at Columbia however. They had worked on the original Yardbirds and expected to sign Jimmy Page's new project. They were too late. When Peter went to meet Clive Davis, the Columbia boss, he had already signed Zeppelin to Atlantic for five years and had already set up the group's own production and publishing companies.

The band played a few more shows in England before setting off for America and they included Manchester College on November 16, 1968, Sheffield University (23), Bath Pavilion (December 16), Exeter City Hall (19), and Fishmongers Hall, London (20). They made their US debut on December 26 in Denver, Colorado.

In the New Year they played at the home of underground music, the Fillmore West in San Francisco, with Country Joe and The Fish. The album was sent in advance of release to various radio stations which helped pave the way for the band's arrival in town. They were getting less than two thousand dollars a night for their first gigs, but it was all good exposure and already the reviews were pouring in, mostly ecstatic. By March the album was in the Top Twenty, and they had toured the

East Coast towns with two spots at the Fillmore East in New York. By May the album was Number Ten in the US charts and stayed hovering around for over a year.

Back home, the band were still trying to convince the lethargic public of their existence and they toured heavily throughout March and April with a scheduled trip to Scandinavia thrown in. Also in March they made a rare TV appearance on the *How It Is* show, where they played *Communication Breakdown*, the greatest two minutes of high energy since *My Generation*. Out on the road they were still committed to small clubs – the Marquee, Mother's in Birmingham and Klooks Kleek, Hampstead, literally a tiny room above a pub.

Their TV spot had only come about because the Flying Burrito Brothers had dropped out of the BBC show at the last minute and had to be replaced. By April the album was at last a Top Ten hit in Britain. It was given rave reviews, particularly in the Melody Maker where the headline blazed: 'Jimmy Page triumphs! Led Zeppelin is a gas'. We added: 'Their material does not rely on obvious blues riffs, although when they do play them they avoid the emaciated feebleness of most so-called British blues bands.'

In March I met Jimmy for an interview and he told me: 'We've been very successful in the States. We can hardly believe it! At most of the places we play we seem to get mass hysteria. In Boston I noticed all the boys in the front row were beating their heads in time (an early reference to the phenomenon of head banging). When we started the group we only had enough material for fifty minutes, but this extended to two hours. We're all feeling happy, especially about the American reaction which is more than we ever dreamed could happen. I'm looking forward to playing at the Newport Jazz Festival. It's a great honour because there will be people like Muddy Waters and Stan Getz there. What's so good about the States is they can mix so many different styles. I saw a concert with Cecil Taylor who is as far out as you can get, on the same bill with Richie Havens and the Yardbirds. That's three completely different styles and they were all accepted by the audience at the Fillmore.'

Jimmy waxed lyrical about the artistic freedom America then offered. 'Music is part of their life. In England a club is more a place for kids to meet and they are not really interested in the music, which makes it hard for a lot of new groups to get off the ground.'

The American way of life made a tremendous impression on all young British musicians who were more in touch with it than most politicians and journalists, and certainly more than the average man in the street in the days before cheap, mass air travel.

'There are so many things about America I like,' said Jimmy. 'Things you take for granted like having a good telephone system. And they don't force you to go to bed at 10.30pm by switching off all the TV programmes and stopping the trains.'

I hadn't seen the band for some months at that stage. Would they be joining a supposed trend and turn down their volume? 'No – we're getting louder,' promised Jim. 'Our drummer is amazingly loud. I come off stage with my ears singing after a set.'

That month Zeppelin took part in historic filming sessions at Staines which resulted in the pioneer rock movie *Super Session* which also featured Eric Clapton, Stephen Stills, Buddy Miles, the Modern Jazz Quartet, Roland Kirk, Buddy Guy, Colosseum and Glenn 'Fernando' Campbell, the steel guitar man.

On April 24 they returned to the States for their second tour and opened at the Fillmore West on April 24 alongside Brian Auger and Julie Driscoll who supported them on most of the tour dates. This time Zeppelin were undisputed bill-toppers and their fees had quadrupled. To give value for money they played a two hour set with *Train Kept A Rollin'* their opening number. The tour lasted well into June, an exhausting marathon which was but the first of many.

They came home again in June and played at Bath Festival where 12,000 fans came to see them at their biggest ever British concert. The following night they played at the Royal Albert Hall at the pop proms. It was part of their first nationwide British tour and they were supported by Blodwyn Pig and Liverpool Scene. After the tour they began work on *Led Zeppelin II*, but had to return to America for more concerts in ever larger venues. They even played at the Newport, Baltimore and Philadelphia jazz festivals. In New York they played to a crowd of 21,000. The group were constantly upstaging their American partners on the bill, and bands like The Doors and Iron Butterfly were all blown off by Zeppelin in full cry. By August the band were earning over thirty thousand dollars for a gig, their income boosted by insisting on a percentage of the door money.

The tour finished at the end of August and then the band took time off for a holiday, Jimmy heading for a totally different environment in Morocco, where he fully expected to get arrested for his long hair and general appearance. Once safely back home he got to work on the new album which had been written mostly in hotel rooms between concerts. It was finished off at Olympic Studios.

On October 12th they played at the Lyceum Ballroom in the Strand. As a keen student of airship history I knew this was almost fifty-four years to the day since the German airship Zeppelin LZ15, commanded by Joachim Breithaupt, had led a raid on London in which he had bombed the Lyceum. I also discovered that during the First World War German school children used to sing 'Fly Zeppelin, Help us in the war. Fly to England. England shall be destroyed by fire. Fly Zeppelin!' Jimmy

Page was most amused by all this, especially as Eva Von Zeppelin, a relative of the airship designer, had raged against the group using the family name. 'They may be world famous' she said, 'but a couple of shrieking monkeys are not going to use a privileged family name without permission.' Jimmy retaliated by saying they would rename the band The Nobs when they played in Copenhagen, where she was based.

'The whole thing is absurd,' he told me. 'The first time we played in Copenhagen she turned up and tried to stop a TV show. She couldn't of course, but we invited her to meet us to show we were nice young lads. We calmed her down, but on leaving the studio, she saw our LP cover of an airship in flames and she exploded! I had to run and hide. She just blew her top. So – we are shrieking moneys now! But she is really quite a nice person.

'They wanted us to fly in an airship over Montreux, Switzerland once. That's tempting fate isn't it? I told them to fly without us and say we were inside.'

I saw the band perform at Bath Festival where their impact on fans was by now obvious even to the most irascible cynic. Jimmy played guitar with his violin bow and the audience kept yelling out 'How many more times!' which puzzled me, until I remembered it was the last track on the album, and not an expression of impatience. All such confusion was swept away by the time I went to the Lyceum performance. Fading memories of those far off days were recently revived when a German bootleg album (cheekily labelled Grant Musik) of the concert was released. The aural evidence, although not particularly well recorded, showed the band to be almost frantic with energy, and tremendously exciting, although they benefitted in later years by learning how to relax and pace out their set.

The concert was promoted by Tony Smith and the group were paid one of the highest fees ever for a single performance by one band in the U.K. Zeppelin played some of the numbers from the next album including *Heart Breaker* and *What Is And What Should Never Be*.

A few days beforehand I had been sitting at my inkstained and battered desk at the Melody Maker office when the editor Jack Hutton suddenly barked in a heavy Scots accent across a recently constructed partition (known as the Berlin Wall), 'How would you like to go to America? With Led Zeppelin?'

After some six years on Melody Maker my furthest trip west thus far in the cause of rock 'n' roll had been to the Ricky Tick Club in Windsor. I was thrilled. After mad scrambles to get a visa (the queues were smaller in those days), I rushed to get a taxi to Euston Station to meet the band. They were due to play at the prestigious Carnegie Hall in New York. As a jazz fan, the first LP I ever bought (and still treasure) was the Benny

54

Goodman Carnegie Hall concert. The sound of Gene Krupa's drums on *Sing Sing Sing* from that legendary affair had set in train the chain of events that led me to the MM and now led me to Led Zeppelin and Carnegie Hall. It made all the years of interviewing the Rockin' Berries and Herman's Hermits seem worthwhile.

It was on Thursday October 16, 1969 that I made my way to Euston and that autumn afternoon in London stays in my memory as a kind of dream. The Americans had only recently landed on the moon, and as far as I was concerned a trip to America was an infinitely more exciting prospect than a lunar landing.

I met Robert Plant and John Bonham for the first time outside the station, clutching my passport, tickets and a box of harmonicas for Robert. I stood waiting for them to emerge from the mass of commuters. Their train was late but eventually Robert and John appeared. I wrote later: 'They were filled with the cheeriness of musicians on their way to earn a few dollars more – a hundred thousand dollars to be precise.'

Packed into the taxi we sped towards London Airport and Robert, a mass of golden curls falling over his face, chattered about the reaction towards Zeppelin's success. 'I think a lot of people in Britain have been against us for some reason. I just can't understand it, but they say we are a made-up manufactured group because we were successful right away. But we just got together in the same way all groups get together. I don't see how some magazines can call us a hype.

'When we went over to America for the first time last Christmas we found we weren't even billed and we got a bit depressed. But Atlantic Records began pushing out LPs in the towns where we were due to play so people heard us before we arrived.

'People were ready to accept us from the album – it was up to us to prove ourselves on stage. From then on it just grew.'

Robert explained that the new album should have been out but the art work had been held up. 'It's such a drag. But the album should be out in America next week. The tracks were done all over the place, in Los Angeles, New York and London. On one number I put the vocals on a backing track that had been recorded in Atlantic Studios in New York, in a hut in Vancouver.

'It's hard to say how different it is from the first. You can distinguish the voices and the songs are better. The band is better because we have been together longer. The excitement is still there and we also do some quieter things which can be equally effective as groups like Fairport Convention prove. They don't need crescendos all the time.

'On the last album the drum and guitar sound was the same on every track. This one has different sounds for different songs, which are all originals. Really we can't wait to get onto our next album!'

At the airport we met Jimmy Page, John Paul Jones and Peter Grant.

There were fans waiting to see them off and Robert was delighted when one of them gave him a copy of Paul Oliver's book Story Of The Blues which kept him engrossed for the seven hour TWA flight. We travelled first class on a Boeing 707 and as I drank champagne and partook of caviar I gazed at the sun setting over the Atlantic. The group were all very quiet, pausing to chat to fellow passenger Graham Nash and wandering up and down the centre aisle. It was my first trip on anything larger than a BEA Vanguard and I hoped that such tramping about did not upset the trim of the aircraft and plunge us all into the ocean below.

From Kennedy Airport we drove in a huge black limo to the Hilton Hotel in Manhattan, accompanied by their attorney Sid Weiss who made the unforgettable remark about *Led Zeppelin II* being a masterpiece. I felt increasingly overawed. While much the same age as the band, I was impressed by their ease at coping with big business, flattery, adulation and being millionaires at twenty-two. I stared at New York with its huge buildings pressing down and felt I was being mesmerised. But the energy of the city brought me back to life and when I saw the reaction to Zeppelin I felt a sudden pride in the band, like a football fan cheering on his team at an away match.

The rooms at the massive Hilton were remarkably small and I watched with growing disbelief the appalling TV programmes constantly interrupted by crass and banal advertisements. Unbeknown to me the band were attempting to ease the boredom of solitary confinement. The next morning I received a telephone call. Had I enjoyed the night's entertainment? Had things gone . . . well? My blank reaction seemed to induce disappointment.

Later I discovered that a plot had been hatched to send two hookers to my room armed with blue films and whips, but they had been spotted entering the elevator by a hotel detective and had been arrested.

The following day, Friday 17th, I went to visit the Atlantic Studios and watched Les McCann record an album and met Dr John Creux the well known Night Tripper. The Atlantic office, then on Broadway, was buzzing with excitement at the arrival of their latest British group and minions were busily inflating rubber Led Zeppelins, made in Japan. I heard members of the staff shouting: 'Led Zeppelin and The Who are the two biggest acts in America. It's like the Monkees never existed.'

I heard that the band were due to be paid fifteen thousand dollars a night for the tour dates which followed the Carnegie Hall show. A percentage of the gate would bring them twenty thousand dollars a night for fourteen days.

Tension mounted as zero hour neared. The show was being presented by Howard Stein, and Carnegie Hall rarely allowed rock on its premises. The hall was then being threatened with closure despite having been recently restored with new gilt decor and plush red seats. It

56

was a beautiful old building and rightly famous throughout the world. It seemed a scandal that it should be destined to make way for yet another concrete and glass tower. Mercifully, wiser counsels prevailed.

I purchased a programme which proved a remarkably low key affair, containing simply a mention of the band's name, an advertisement for *Led Zeppelin II* and an article about Beethoven by George Bernard Shaw.

Soon I found myself standing on the famous stage during the afternoon sound check. To my delight John Bonham understood and shared my emotions. After all, this was the spot were in 1938 Gene Krupa hammered his tom toms and launched a thousand aspiring drummers.

'This is it lads,' said Bonzo, eyeing his drum kit as the audience began to file in early and take their seats. 'Gene Krupa and Buddy Rich – they've all played here. So I'd better be good tonight!'

There were quite a few fellow British musicians in the dressing room on hand to lend their support and drink some champagne. Chris Wood of Traffic, who had been working with Dr. John appeared at my side while I stood in the wings, and Screaming Lord Sutch in a yellow jacket, wearing an 'I'm Backing Britain' badge revealed all the local news and gossip.

Suddenly someone discovered that Robert had left his box of harmonicas behind in the hotel so I volunteered to nip back and get them. The Hilton was literally just round the corner. But they wouldn't let me walk the streets at night. The new phenomenon of mugging had just begun to spread through American cities and arrived in Britain (along with credit cards, breakfast TV and fast food) a few years later. They would take no chances and insisted that the Cadillac be brought out from the underground car park and I be driven half a block to the hotel. I would cheerfully have carried half their PA on my back, such was the feeling of patriotism when I saw the reaction to the band once the concert was underway.

From the moment of their 8.30pm kick off I stood at the side of the stage (they had forgotten to get me a ticket), and watched fascinated for the duration of their two hour set. The band played with a sustained drive and intensity never encountered before in rock, even in the heyday of Cream and Hendrix, only three short years before.

They were setting standards that would be emulated ad infinitum by countless groups in the years ahead. In my review I wrote: 'They have a sense of the dramatic and a professionalism that leaves the impression of reserves of ideas and power. They play hard, fast and furious. But they are in control.'

Huge cheers greeted the band as Robert ran on stage dressed in black, followed by Jimmy in white satin trousers, John Bonham in a leather hat and John Paul Jones in a red outfit. The battering snare drum introduction to *Communication Breakdown* made me blink and the guitar sound

57

on *I Can't Quit You* was almost erotic in its intensity.

Soon the fans, teenage boys and girls leapt to their feet, reaching out to grab at Zeppelin and shake them by the hands, a practice I'd never seen in England where most fans were content to stand at the back of a hall, gazing morosely into their beer. I was frankly amazed at the reaction of the New Yorkers. I had no idea that Americans could develop such affection and admiration for a British group so quickly.

We knew that they had loved The Beatles, but to show such hero worship for our lads from the Marquee required a swift mental readjustment. In America rock music was important and a nationwide growth industry, not just a pub recreation for moderate stakes on a par with darts, ludo and cribbage.

Silence fell when Jimmy sat down to play a quiet acoustic solo. 'He's a masterful guitar player' a voice breathed in my ear. It was recording engineer Eddie Kramer.

The solo began with a basic theme and worked through a series of inventive ideas. All the years of frustration, the eight bar breaks and solos permitted during sessions were swept away and replaced by new found freedom of expression.

There were other instrumental delights. John Bonham made good his promise to be on form. He played a thirty minute drum solo in which he flew round the kit with a speed and brute strength that was astounding. He played with the same sort of high speed snare drum single stroke rolls that Buddy Rich had featured on the same stage during concerts in the Fifties.

John played with sticks, beaters, even his hands and the applause came in waves of enthusiasm. After this (I never saw John play quite so fast again incidentally), the atmosphere was electric. Robert leapt across the stage singing his heart out and standing on tip toe in an apparent effort to reach even higher notes. The ushers tried to restrain the crowd, but there was no violence. John Paul Jones' bass set up the familiar riff of *Summertime Blues*, which they played as their encore. Of all the many occasions I saw Zeppelin in action, there were few that had quite the zip and magic of that show. It was probably because it was the first of a tour when the band were at a pitch of excitement in making their first impact in the States, but I also felt it had something to do with the aura of Carnegie Hall which seems to inspire musicians of each generation whatever their musical style.

After the Benny Goodman concerts of 1938 somebody said: 'It was too damn bad they didn't record the whole thing.' Back in '38 somebody had, with a single microphone. Alas, there were no recorders on hand in October 1969.

After the show I went with the band to a Jewish delicatessen on Sixth Avenue and asked Robert and Jimmy about the reaction. 'You should

58

see the kids in Boston or Detroit,' said Robert still drenched in sweat and blemished with an unfortunate rash that broke out during the first set: 'You can control the audience if you are reasonable with them and don't chuck them off stage too violently.'

Said John Paul Jones: 'We've played over three hours without a break in Boston. You get to the stage where you don't want to get off stage!'

Said Jimmy: 'After doing such a long show you don't really feel like repeating it the same evening, especially after a long flight. But nervous energy sustains you.'

I attempted to find out *why* Zeppelin had been such a success.

'Everybody in the group is strong. It's not like some groups where you have one stand out and the rest are passengers. When people see our shows they can come back again and find out some different facet of our ability. John Paul Jones for example is playing amazing bass things – he's frightening.'

One of the most impressive parts of the show had been Jimmy's solo called *White Summer*. Said Jimmy: 'There are all different bits on it. There's *Black Mountain* off the first album. I just play . . . improvise until the enthusiasm lags. It's the sort of thing I sit at home and play all night on an acoustic. There are Indian and folk influences in *White Summer* which give you a chance to show you can play all sorts of things as well as the blues. Somebody in the audience offered me a bottle of champagne after I played it – and that's how involved they are in music over there. They are involved in England as well but they don't make it so apparent.'

The next day Zeppelin left New York for Detroit. I sat in my limo outside the Hilton waiting for a chauffeur to drive me to the airport and back to London. An elderly lady poked her wizened face through the open window. 'Are you rich?' she demanded, making a rude gesture with her fingers and nose. 'No, not really,' I said. 'Huh, gotta be a Limey,' she muttered and stomped off.

On October 22 *Led Zeppelin II* was released in the States with advance orders of 400,000 and within a couple of weeks was at Number Two in the album charts. Then began the mysterious affair of the band's refusal to put out singles. The album track *Whole Lotta Love* was an obvious hit, and indeed became the anthem most associated with Zeppelin and part of the soundtrack of the Seventies. In November the five minute track was edited down to a single length and pushed out to American radio stations. It got into the charts naturally enough and by January was at Number Four. Back home there were demands for the single to be released in England as well. But Peter Grant insisted that no single by the band could be issued. The reason, baffling on the face of it, became clear. The album was selling like a single anyway and there was no need to cream off one of the best tracks. And Jimmy Page didn't like the idea

59

of their being pressurised into putting out singles which at that time were regarded as representative of only the most naff forms of pop music.

In December I went to the Savoy Hotel where a curious ceremony took place. Mrs Gwyneth Dunwoody, Parliamentary Secretary to the Board of Trade, presented the band with a gold and two platinum records for their American sales. There were many chuckles in the background from somewhat inebriated music journalists, including some singularly uncalled for remarks from 'The Beast', Richard Green of Record Mirror. Fortunately Mrs Dunwoody didn't notice the cries of 'get 'em off'. Jimmy Page was late arriving for the ceremony due to an accident on the M4, but afterwards I went with him on a shopping expedition – to buy a new Rolls Royce. I remember the classic experience of entering the showroom in one of London's exclusive squares, and Jimmy, his flowing long hair and flamboyant outfit, and me in my Fleet Street beerstained togs, approaching the smartly dressed salesman. I don't think Jimmy actually said "Ere mate, got a Roller?' but it was pretty close to the same culture clash once graphically described by newly rich Michael Caine.

By now the days of starving, especially for Robert and Bonzo were over. They were all busy buying large houses and farms, while Jimmy was happily ensconced in his unique wooden boathouse by the Thames at Pangbourne. Time off the road and trips back to England were precious to them. John Bonham liked to keep in touch with his roots away from the unreal world of concerts and flights. He got down to such pursuits as decorating and gardening, anything physical with a visible end product. It was not long since he and his wife Pat had been forced to live in a caravan. Said John: 'I was determined that when we had a house and a garden of our own, I would keep them in wonderful shape. I picked up quite a bit about house construction while working on building sites.' He now owned a large house near Stourbridge, Worcestershire.

Robert was not far away on   Jennings Farm, Blakeshall. He liked to get there as much as possible. His car crash had left him feeling groggy and he needed as much rest as possible. But even back at the farm he couldn't escape injury and bad luck. He was doing some repairs to his Aston Martin when the jack broke while he was lying underneath. He was lucky to escape with just cuts and bruises.

On the road Robert attempted to act as calmly as possible and avoid over excitement between shows. 'The worst thing in the world is to rush,' he claimed. 'Being on the road so much has taught me that. All I want to do is sit back and take it easy. The farm calms me down. When I'm away onstage I'm so into it that if I didn't have the farm I'd go mad. The farm is the other end of the scale for me.'

Robert got into farming with the same enthusiasm as Bonzo. He tilled the soil, sowed crops on three acres of land, and tended six milk producing goats. The lifestyle provided a perfect balance. There was nothing like a spot of ploughing to soothe his turbulent emotions.

Robert lived in the rambling old farm house with his wife Maureen, baby daughter Carmen and a dog called Stryder. The farm was set in a leafy glade overlooking a valley and here Robert spent many a happy hour cleaning out the stables.

Despite the yearning for normality, there were times when the band couldn't resist flaunting their newly earned riches, especially when provoked. Rich rock stars were still an unknown quantity as far as the public was concerned. In one incident in Carnaby Street Robert wanted to buy an eight guinea shirt. Although recognised by the staff who produced an LP with his picture on the sleeve, the manager demanded identification from the hairy youth. Robert simply tore up his cheque and stalked out.

On another occasion the band were forced to stop at a late night roadside 'greasy spoon' cafe for a meal, and were the subject of much baiting and ridicule from the regular patrons. At the end of the meal the road crew drove up the front door in the band's huge limo, to collect the stars who left behind a massive tip.

John Bonham marched into a Birmingham car showroom with two suitcases bulging with £10,000 in cash and bought a brand new Maserati. He explained to the startled assistant that the money came from just three dates he'd played in America a couple of days before.

In the midst of the spending sprees, John Bonham also invested in a tiny set of miniature drums for his two-year-old son Jason, who swiftly began playing them with an enthusiasm that was to lead him to create his own career in rock. Said Bonzo in a 1970 interview: 'My son Jason plays. I've got him a little Japanese drum kit made to scale. It's got a 14 inch bass drum. He's got his mother's looks but in character he's just like me. He's always drumming. Even when we go out in the car he takes his sticks to bash on the seats. He hasn't got much technique but he's got a great sense of time. Before the end of Led Zeppelin I'm going to have him on stage with us at the Albert Hall.'

1970 began with a short British tour including a concert at the Royal Albert Hall in London on January 9. A few weeks later on February 1 Robert was involved in the car crash when driving his Jaguar home from a Spirit concert. He had head and facial injuries and a gig in Edinburgh was cancelled.

Led Zeppelin II was by now Number One on both sides of the Atlantic with Whole Lotta Love being given constant radio plays. But the band refused to appear on BBC TV's Top Of The Pops show, which in later years used Whole Lotta Love – in a different version – as its theme tune.

61

In fact they wouldn't make any TV appearances, once again flying in the face of accepted works' customs and practices. Jimmy Page explained: 'I don't think TV people anywhere know how to present a group – especially from the point of getting the sound right. So if viewers can't see and hear us at our best then we'd rather stay off the small screen.'

The band had filmed their Albert Hall concert and an hour and a half of footage must still be rotting somewhere in a vault. Robert, on viewing the rushes, declared the film hilarious, showing them pulling various tortured expressions.

Robert's accident came at a time of feverish activity and said Jimmy: 'Everything was slowed up when Robert had his car accident and he's still in a bad way. We had to cancel some work, although he said he would appear on stage in a wheelchair. We've got a lot of work to do. On our first album we were finding out about each other. For the third I've prepared a lot of acoustic stuff. It's been quite a year for us. I can hardly believe what has happened. Four tours of the States and two platinum albums. There are very powerful astrological forces at work within the band whch I am sure had a lot to do with our success. Robert is a Leo which makes him a perfect leader, with two Capricorns on either side, and a Gemini behind. I'm a Capricorn which speaks for itself – very stubborn with a split personality.'

1970 was a time of great changes. Even the Melody Maker was affected. I had a phone call at home one Sunday afternoon from the editor saying: 'Hello Chris – are you standing up? Then sit down. I'm leaving the Melody Maker and I'm starting a new paper. Do you want to come with me?' The new paper was to be called Sounds. Half the staff, including the tea lady and office boy left the MM to go with the director, ad manager and editor to start the rival paper. After three pay rises in a couple of weeks and promotion, I decided to stay on the Melody Maker which in any case I thought was the best, proved by the fact it could be so successfully copied by both New Musical Express, who relaunched with a rock policy and Sounds.

But I had to prove I was worth the three pay rises and help a paper suffering mortal blows to its morale. Reporters were leaving by the hour and new, innocent and untried faces loomed spottily over the ancient typewriters.

I had been elevated to the rank of features editor. A call came from above, was there any chance of getting an interview with Led Zeppelin? The editor was most anxious to have a three part series that could form the plank of an anti-Sounds campaign. I set off by car to Pangbourne on an unauthorised visit to Jimmy's boathouse, hoping to catch him at home. To my delight he came to the door, invited me in and granted a brace of interviews which were really pleasant chats over a couple of days.

We went around the corner to the local olde worlde tea shoppe. A battered Vauxhall car was rattling through the village as we strolled along the street. The grinning passenger desperately wound down his window to yell at us 'Git yer hair cut.'

'We've made his day,' said Jimmy. It was ironic. He was idolised by millions throughout the world and yet was regarded as an object of ridicule on his own doorstep.

A few yards further on we came across a group of school children, come home from their local seat of learning. 'He's one of THEM!' they tittered. 'Even the kids don't like me,' said Jimmy. 'It's the way their parents bring them up. I suppose it must be the long hair they don't like. Oh no – it's the trousers. That's what's doing it.' Jimmy muttered almost to himself in philosophical fashion as we entered the cafe.

Here the proprietress gazed at us with suspicion but eventually served us with steak and chips. We talked and ate and pondered over the amazing success of Jimmy's venture since the day two years before when he had turned up in the office to announce the new group.

Four million albums sold. Honours for contributions to the nation's exports and industry. Acclaim at Carnegie Hall . . .

'GIT YER HAIR CUT!'

FIVE

FIVE ENCORES FOR ZEPPELIN

A curious calm settled over Zeppelin as the enormous success of their enterprise settled on them like robes of office. They were the best and knew it. The riches that came in a rush were rightfully theirs, earned by dint of toil. And if the money that poured in bred envy and resentment, it should be remembered that it represented only a small amount of the millions sloshing around in an industry that had to be prized open to give up its treasures. Once the middle men had reaped the rewards of artistic endeavour. Now the band, with their manager, Peter Grant, ensured that a much bigger percentage came their way.

Said Peter: 'The days of the promoter giving a few quid to the group as against the money taken on the door has gone. The business was run by managers, agents and promoters, when it was the groups who brought in the money. I thought the musicians should be the people who got the wages.'

Jimmy Page was insistent that the success of the band had come as a surprise to them. 'None of us expected to be this big,' he protested. 'It was a total shock when I heard the second LP was selling faster than the first. It's frightening the way it has snowballed. It wasn't a contrived thing. It was just good luck and good timing.'

It was February 1970 when I went to Jimmy's rambling wooden boathouse beside the Thames. It was a cold but sunny day and I could appreciate the peace of the countryside as much as the occupant. He had

64

a telephone to keep in touch with London, which rang incessantly throughout the day, but outside the front porch was the calming effect of the river filled with swans and ducks. Cows gazed across the water from fields on the opposite bank, and Jimmy had a large white telescope trained on them from the living room.

Jimmy reclined on the arm of a settee, while his girlfriend Charlotte Martin, a French model, made us tea.

'I'm changing my telephone number,' said Jimmy. 'They tell me I should have done it long ago, we get about thirty or forty calls a day. I have been editing tapes for the next LP and you need your wits about you for that. There were interruptions all the time which made it a day long job. I'm not ex-directory and you can't tell people you really are busy. They think you are just trying to get rid of them.

'All this started within the last six months. I bought the house about two and a half years ago when I was with The Yardbirds. There hasn't been time to decorate being away in the States so much, but you wouldn't have believed the scene when I moved in.

'The previous owner had great garlands of plastic flowers everywhere. She even had a barrow in the corner decorated with plastic flowers. It was like a Norseman's funeral when we threw all the flowers onto the river.'

We wandered around the interior of the house which revealed a surprising number of oddly shaped rooms and passages, and down below the ground floor was a huge room housing the central heating, a dismantled antique bed, considerable quantities of junk and a motor launch bobbing about in an inlet, waiting for the summer.

'This is the tub,' said Jimmy. It was too cold for boating expeditions so we carried on to the top of the house where under the low ceilings lay a muddled pile of paintings, records, model trains and books. In particular there were books about magic and the writings of Aleister Crowley. His interest in the occult was not unique. A great many people, not just in the music business, were interested in alternative sciences, everything from astrology to numerology. Jimmy was just as much interested in antiques and fine art.

By the time we had concluded our tour there was hardly any time left for an interview, so I went back for a second visit. Jimmy was in a cheery mood. Builders were carrying out some overdue structural improvements. His manager had just presented him with a Bentley, Jimmy having decided against a Rolls, and the ancient penny peep-show he had installed in his bedroom had started to work properly.

Jimmy told me he had spent three hours a day practising the guitar to get in shape for the summer tours that lay ahead. 'Unfortunately there has been a great lack of practice in the last year or so. I play a long improvised solo to get fluency and then a difficult phrase to see if I can

65

pull it off. I'd like to be able to play the piano. It sounds strange. I can play guitar with finger style independence but I can't play piano. I'd like to play violin but that's not as easy as it looks. When I use violin bow on guitar it's not just a gimmick as people think. It's because some great sounds come out. You can employ legitimate bowing techniques and gain new scope and depth. The only drawback is that a guitar has a flat neck as opposed to a violin's curved neck which is a bit limiting.'

The band were due to start a European tour on February 21 followed by trips to America. I asked Jimmy how British fans would fare. He revealed they were toying with a noble idea that eventually came to nothing. 'We want to do some free concerts this year. We may be doing one at Glastonbury at the time of the Summer Solstice. But I'm not so sure about Hyde Park. I know in the States they can't have any more because of the Stones thing at Altamont. Everybody is frightened which is a shame because this type of concert is valuable and legitimate.'

At the time the music press had been awash with rumours of the band splitting up, so I had to ask Jimmy if any of it was true, even though I guessed that most of the rumours had been started deliberately to undermine the band's success. 'There's no reason to split up. There is nothing inherent musically in Led Zeppelin to harm or destroy it. There is variety, great freedom and no restrictions on the players whatsoever. It's good from a head point of view. In our band everybody respects each other. Everybody plays something to knock each other out.

'I can't see any split coming. People say to us – 'Now you are established, when are you going to break up?' That's a terrible attitude. I heard recently that Crosby, Stills and Nash are going to split up. Fans develop loyalty to a group and that becomes impossible when groups break up so often. We'll carry on and stick together – like The Beatles and The Stones.'

The band set off for Copenhagen where they did indeed call themselves The Nobs, as Jimmy promised, then in March started their fifth American tour with twenty-seven dates lined up. The tour was marred by violent incidents and hostility. The success of the band and their reputation as hell raisers had lured the lunatic fringe – not just fans but policemen and red necks who resented their long hair and money, couldn't understand what all the fuss was about, felt alienated by the turn of events and somehow felt provoked. In restaurants the band were treated just as blacks had been treated in the South, not being served, and made to feel unwelcome. In Texas a redneck shouted abuse and pulled a gun on them. Eventually they hired a posse of eight bodyguards to keep them out of danger, while police and audiences slugged it out.

But it wasn't all bad news. In April they were made honorary citizens of Memphis, Tennessee and fans began the practice of lighting candles

66

which they held up in moving displays during the concerts. In later years the candles and matches were replaced by butane cigarette lighters.

After the tour finished in Las Vegas, Robert collapsed from exhaustion and it was decided that if they were ever to compose and finish the third album they would have to leave the madhouse of America and find one of the world's safer spots. Thus in May Jimmy and Robert went to Wales and a secluded cottage called 'Bron-y-Aur' in Snowdonia. The Welsh name meant Golden Breast and Robert had known about the spot since childhood, when he visited it with his parents. Jimmy had never been there before he went off on the trip, armed with guitars and recorders. But they weren't just intent on writing songs in the country, they wanted to enjoy themselves as well. So they took a couple of roadies with them who helped keep the log fires burning. Said Jimmy: 'As the nights wore on the guitars came out and numbers were being written. It wasn't really planned as a working holiday but some songs did come out of it.'

They certainly appreciated the privacy and beauty of the natural surroundings and later Robert bought the cottage which was celebrated in Zeppelin song titles.

The music for the new album was much more varied and relaxed than on the first two block blusters and the aim was to show the different directions the band could go in, while holding on to their basically heavy feel. Said Robert: 'We want to get more variety into the act. We're not in one particular bag.'

The album was released on October 5th and featured an unusual sleeve with a rotating cardboard wheel, designed by Richard Drew, a fine arts lecturer from Leeds Polytechnic. It resembled an old fashioned seed catalogue but instead of flowers and vegetables featured juxtapositions of surreal flying objects, from aircraft to butterflies. Artistically it wasn't particularly attractive but at least it was clearly identified with the name of the band on the cover.

I went back to the boathouse one Saturday evening to hear the album and discuss the tracks with Jimmy, but only after we had played his own choice of music which included albums by The Cream, Jody Grind, Tony Williams and Don Ellis. Later we talked about the origin of the new songs and he hinted at the band's musical future and the content of *Led Zeppelin IV* which was then on the 'drawing board'.

The first track was *Immigrant Song*, which I had heard being put together in the studios and featured a powerful drum riff from Bonham. Said Jimmy: 'That's a voice at the beginning incidentally which somebody has said is a wailing guitar. On stage this number has already developed into a much longer thing, with a full instrumental passage. The hiss at the beginning is a tape build up, then John Bonham comes in. It's not really tape hiss. It's echo feed-back. Robert wrote the lyrics.'

Friends: 'Again Robert wrote the words. He did them all except on *Tangerine*. The idea was to get an Indian style with the strings. The string players were not Indian however and we had to make some on the spot changes. John Paul Jones wrote an incredible string arrangement for this and Robert shows his great range – incredibly high. He's got a lot of different sides to his voice which come across here. A friend came into the studio during the recording and it was bloody loud and he had to leave. He said: "You've really done something evil!"'

Celebration Day: 'The reason the voice is alone is the tape got crinkled in the studio and wouldn't go through the heads, so the end got ruined. But it worked out all right by using the idea of bringing the synthesiser down in pitch to the voice. Why Celebration? It's just saying "I'm happy," that's all.'

Since I've Been Loving You: 'This was a live track. John Paul plays organ and foot bass pedals at the same time. My guitar solo could have been better but you know, you are never satisfied with a performance. There are those lucky musicians who can play perfectly every time. On these types of numbers John decides his own drum beat to play. We might occasionally suggest the use of conga drums on a particular number but he always fixes his own beat.'

Out On The Tiles: 'This is Bonzo's riff. Originally we had a set of lyrics to go with this relating to a night going out on the tiles.'

Gallows Pole: 'A traditional song which stems from Leadbelly. I first found it by Fred Gerlac. He was one of the first white people on Folkways Records to get involved in Leadbelly. We have completely rearranged it and changed the verse. Robert wrote a new set of lyrics. That's John Paul on mandolin and bass and I'm playing banjo, six string acoustic, twelve string and electric guitar. The bloke swinging on the gallows pole is saying wait for his relatives to arrive. The drumming builds up nicely!'

Tangerine: 'That's commonly known as a false start. It was a tempo guide and it seemed like a good idea to leave it in – at the time. I was trying to keep the tempo down a bit, I'm not so sure now it was a good idea. Everybody asks what the hell is going on. I did the pedal steel guitar and Robert does the harmonies as well as the lead vocals.

That's The Way: 'This was written in Wales, where Robert and I stayed at the cottage. It was one of those days after a long walk and we were setting back to the cottage. We had a guitar with us. It was a tiring walk coming down a ravine and we stopped and sat down. I played the tune and Robert sang a verse straight off. We had a tape recorder with us . . . that sounds a bit strange . . . but it was part of the kit . . . and we got the tune down.' Jimmy emphasised that it wasn't recorded in Wales and in fact sessions for the album were held at Headley Grange, a country house in Hampshire, where they had recorded with a mobile studio throughout May.

Bron-Y-Aur Stomp: 'That's an acoustic bass, not a double bass. It's like an acoustic guitar with a big body. This has got the rattling of a kitchen sink – everything in it. We overdubbed Bonham on castanets and spoons.'

Hats Off To (Roy) Harper: This came about from a jam Robert and I had one night. There is a whole tape of us bashing different blues things. Robert had been playing harmonica through the amp, then he used it to sing through. It's supposed to be a sincere hats off to Roy because he's really a talented bloke, who's had a lot of problems.' Roy Harper, the electric folk singer had impressed the band when they were billed together on the 1969 Bath Festival.

I asked Jimmy which was his favourite cut on the album. The album had received mixed reviews, some critics considering it the band's best album thus far, while others thought it too weak and diffuse without enough rockers. Said Jimmy: 'I like *Gallows Pole* but there are others – the point is we had seventeen tracks to choose from to put on the album. Some were written out at the cottage. Some show different stages of development. There was a lot like our early stuff – pretty powerful. And John Paul Jones wrote a piece which was all piano, which would have related to what's coming up in the future. The album was to get across more versatility and use more combinations of instruments. The next one will be just one long track on one side with these combinations of instruments, mandolin, banjo and so on. It would last about twenty-five minutes with instrumental sections. It's still in the planning stages.'

As it turned out the twenty-five minute epic never materialised but promised Jimmy: 'We'll never stop doing the heavy things, because that comes out of us naturally when we play. But – there is another side to us. The new album is totally different from the others and I see that's obviously a new direction. The fourth album should be our best, and if it isn't, well we might as well give up and retire with red faces. I haven't read any of the reviews but people have got to give the LP a reasonable hearing.

'Everybody in the band is going through some changes. There are changes in the playing and in the lyrics. Robert is really getting involved in his lyric writing.'

I asked where Jimmy had got the idea for the cover. 'It was my idea to have a revolving wheel. I remembered those old gardening catalogues. You'd turn it to 'roses' and find out what kind of manure to use. There's a lot more to see on the wheel. When you get fed up with the LP there is the added pleasure of ripping the cover apart to find out what's on the rest of the wheel.'

Jimmy referred to the cover again later in another interview and said

'There was some misunderstanding with the artist – who is in fact very good, but had not been correctly briefed – and we ended up on top of a deadline with a teeny-boppish cover which I think was a compromise.'

In June the band played a couple of concerts in Iceland and turned down offers to play concerts in America worth 200,000 dollars so that they could play at the Bath Festival, the biggest event in the British calendar apart from the Isle Of Wight Festival. I drove to the festival with friends armed with a cine camera. But instead of filming the acts, I used up all the Super Eight colour film clowning around on a disused railway track that we found en route. However one of our number, photographer Barrie Wentzell, took some superb pictures of the band in action at what was to prove one of the most memorable of Zeppelin's British concerts and certainly one they regarded with pleasure.

Said Robert: 'We knew it was going to be a crucial thing. We went on and knew the next three hours were going to be the ones, as far as holding our heads high. We weren't into it until the acoustic number when we all had a chance to sit down and take a look around. Then it was like clockwork. We looked at each other and heard it was sounding good.'

There were some 200,000 fans at the Shepton Mallet grounds in Somerset on Sunday June 28 and the band came on around sunset to gain the maximum atmosphere and excitement. The band played tremendously well against the unglamorous backdrop of a corrugated iron stage. Jimmy appeared wearing a yokel's hat and a straggly beard and his knee length overcoat with massive lapels. He looked like he was auditioning for The Wurzels.

As the fans rose to give them an ovation, Robert told them: 'We've been away a lot in America and we thought it might be a bit dodgy coming back. It's great to be home!' They played for over three hours, blues, rock and pure Zeppelin and John played a massive drum solo. I wrote in my review: 'The crowd went wild demanding encore after encore . . . a total of five!'

Although my film camera was out of action, there were plenty trying to record and even video tape the group at Bath. Apparently Peter Grant threw water into one lot of expensive video tape equipment, although I didn't see it happen. Years later bootleg recordings of the concert did come onto the market and the group were quite interested to hear the results. But Peter took every step possible to prevent tapes being circulated and was most annoyed with the music press for even mentioning them. He told the Melody Maker: 'As far as I know there can be no tapes of Led Zeppelin available. After hearing some time ago that there was going to be an attempt to bootleg tapes of the band, I flew to America to retrieve all the tapes and we know of nothing in existence that can be issued.'

70

Not long after the Bath shows I was invited to go on tour with the band in Germany and this time I would be able to see them in action night after night. This time I took my cine camera with a film in it, and took shots of the group as they travelled by train from city to city, and even on stage in Berlin. I was delighted when the film – silent of course – actually came out despite the darkness in the massive Berlin sports hall. The stage lighting was sufficiently bright for me to get shots of Jimmy swinging his guitar neck around, Bonzo steadfastly pounding his cymbals and tom toms, and Robert wiggling his bottom. I must say that as a silent percursor to *The Song Remains The Same* it wasn't half bad.

Travelling with the band was a unique experience. It was all very well penning reviews from the comfort of Fleet Street. This was rock 'n' roll as hard graft.

I spent five days on the road with them in cars, trains, jets, hotels and dressing rooms. Because of their success they were going through a period when they were under a barrage of now long forgotten criticism, but which mostly tried to ferment trouble within the band. 'We have our rows sure,' said Jimmy. 'But we get on very well, even more so just lately. People just like to have snidey goes at us now and then.'

I was most impressed by the considered and adult way they went about their business. I saw no evidence of rows, only high spirits and during the long hours of travel, an air of solitude descended on the four men and their manager, as they contemplated the nightly concerts which was when the band really came alive. And later they could unwind after the shows at German night clubs where the heat and noise was often louder than at their concerts.

I wrote later: 'They were besieged with autograph hunters and pressmen, faced with audiences of up to 10,000 a night which had to be turned on afresh, and played, laughed and drank without so much as a donner und blitzen. They broke attendance records and still managed to keep the crowds relatively peaceful and content in a country where water hoses and dogs are not unknown.'

The biggest audience and what I thought was their best performance was at Frankfurt Festhall on July 11 when 11,000 fans demanded three encores. The trip began with a bumpy flight from London to Du''sseldorf on a BEA Super One 11 jet. Heavy cloud made the trip seem like a roller coaster ride. Immediately on take off John Bonham lurched to the toilet in the tail – to be sick I was informed. He hated flying and it gave me an inkling into the soft interior behind the image of Bonzo the tough hellraiser. Most of his bravado and heavy drinking stemmed from either boredom or nerves and worry. After all, with the possible exception of Robert, his was the most physical activity on stage each night and sometimes his hands were a mass of blisters and he even drew blood as he swiped with his bare hands at cymbals during his solo.

71

As we flew through the murk above Europe I talked to John Paul Jones. 'They can be hard audiences in Germany,' he warned.

'It's only the second time we have been there. We did Beat Club which must be the best TV show in Europe. They say we are big there – but you can never tell. I reckon we sell well all over Europe.'

Perhaps the flight unnerved them. It certainly caused me to feel the same way as Bonzo, but then I had managed to pack in some thirty flights myself over the previous few years, everything from two seaters and RAF transports to trans-Atlantic Boeings. I'd once taken off from Liverpool airport in a Dakota when the groundcrew had forgotten to shut the door and were running alongside trying to slam it as we taxied down the runway. So this flight seemed no worse than usual. But a silence fell over the passengers. Robert became immersed in Country Life, as befits a gentleman farmer, and Jimmy read a book about the life of poet and wallpaper designer William Morris.

We arrived at Düsseldorf and the trek around German cities enabled us all to see the German miracle first hand. Everything, in comparison to Britain, looked finished. The building work was all done and people were getting on with enjoying themselves. I was particularly impressed by the way the older generation were so well dressed. At home pensioners and the elderly were all (and still are) invariably shabby and under-nourished. The average elderly German in smart suits and outfits, looked like well-off executives.

We checked into the Intercontinental Hotel where nobody batted an eyelid at our appearance. The Germans seemed not only tolerant of English eccentricity but rather welcomed it as light relief. I remember one German hotel receptionist (who of course spoke perfect English) being most concerned and amused at our attempt to decimalise our ancient coinage.

The band certainly presented a striking sight. Robert had shoulder-length golden hair and a moustache and looked like a Viking prince. John Paul Jones wore Lil' Abner dungarees, and Bonzo had a black moustache and black leather jacket that made him resemble a menacing Visigoth. Jimmy wore his yokel's hat and was permanently clutching an antique mirror and table he had collected and carted around with him for safe keeping.

When we left the hotel (where I had spent the entire afternoon drinking with fellow journalist Allan McDougall), I noted that Jimmy was clutching a towel: 'Going swimming?' I inquired.

'No – this is a curtain I wear on stage,' he explained.

'It's curtains for him and granny's knickers for me,' said Robert twisting around to show off a fetching satin shirt billowing around his torso. We arrived at the Sporthall and in the dressing room the band began to show nerves once more. This surprised me. They were so

72

popular. So big. So powerful. And there was Bonham, silent and edgy. It was like the countdown to a big fight. Jimmy broke some of the tension by plugging his guitar into a small amplifier and tuning up with John Paul who was giving vent to some wild hill billy music on mandolin. John Paul and Jimmy really seemed to enjoy a country hoe down and I wondered what the German fans we could hear baying faintly in the distance would think of such music. At last the signal came. They streamed out of the tiny harshly lit dressing room and headed up the stairs towards the stage set up at one end of the dark, cavernous hall.

Each night it was the same. As soon as the first notes of *Immigrant Song* had been blasted out – proving that the PA was working – they could smile and relax and get on with the job. The aim was to grab the attention, keep the ranks of teenagers happy, keep them as quiet as possible during the acoustic set and quieter numbers and then build them towards a musical climax where the cheers would prove that the music had worked. Without those cheers the whole exercise would have been pointless. Rock – all rock and not just Zeppelin's music – lived or died by its ability to communicate and arouse. The nameless worry that one night it might not work, was probably more important than all the fame and money. A failed concert would be a crushing blow to morale and seriously undermine their relationships and mutual trust in the project. Fortunately it never happened, certainly never when I was there.

On the first night of that German tour of long ago, they played well – but not brilliantly. There were fewer people than had been expected. A mere four thousand instead of seven thousand. It turned out there were a thousand politically motivated youths outside demanding free admission.

When the mob were refused entry they took to smashing windows and caused four thousand marks worth of damage. The German promoter, a pleasant and considerate gentleman, Fritz Rau, was very upset and took me on a tour of the damage. 'After nine pm we let them in although 1,500 refused to buy tickets, even when we reduced them to six marks from twelve. But they think all concerts should be free. Edgar Broughton came here and said all music should be free. It's a nice idea but the kids here don't understand about the cost of bringing over a group, and with all the damage we probably won't be able to have pop concerts in this hall again.'

In the dressing room I found an attendant explaining to Robert how they controlled the crowds. 'The police use the sheep dogs instead of the sticks.'

'But the kids don't come for trouble surely,' said a bewildered Plant.

'Yes – and we use the sheep dogs!'

But inside the hall the majority of fans listened peacefully to the two

73

hour show and applauded vigorously if not quite ecstatically.

The next day after much sleep, I set off in a car with Jimmy and Peter in search of antiques. It was Jimmy's great passion at the time and he had learned much about them from Peter who was a considerable authority on the subject. We found a flea market which I thought contained more fleas than objects of art nouveau. It was on the outskirts of town and looked like a rubbish dump, piled high with grandfather clocks, ancient cash registers, gramophones and books. I was surprised to find old Nazi literature openly displayed, magazines which I assumed would have been burned by the Allies. But Adolf was still there in 1970, casting his baleful glare up from the counters.

This was where Jimmy bought the previously mentioned table and mirror which he carried around and which caused much consternation among Pan Am airline officials, who were not wholly convinced by the idea of the objects occupying a seat to themselves in the name of 'Mr. Carson'. Peter also insisted on two seats for himself, to give him room on the cramped seating offered on the Boeing 737 'City Jet', and when this wasn't available there were invariably American grumbles versus English oaths.

That night's concert was in Essen which proved to be the noisiest of the four I attended in Germany. Jimmy gave up trying to play his beloved acoustic guitar and Robert had to plead for the front rows to sit down and listen. 'Christians to the lions,' said Jimmy as they went past me on their way to the stage, and a storm of whistles. Bonzo was more direct. 'You noisy load of buggers!' he yelled at them.

The Grugehalle was a huge impersonal building where the fans crawled ant like across the vast cold and concrete floor. 'We have a problem,' said Robert. 'If you are going to make a noise, we might as well go away – so shut up!' He scolded them like children and was greeted with cheers. Despite this as they went into the eerie introduction to *Dazed And Confused*, a bottle whizzed on stage just as Jimmy was beginning to bow his guitar. Next came a shower of firecrackers. The band played on and pretended not to notice.

Musically they played far better than on the previous night and Jimmy's guitar was flowing with inventive ideas. Robert sang and played harmonica with vibrant passion, shifting in mood from the blues to gentle caressing ballads.

John Bonham's solo was staggering. I was able to watch it each night from a variety of angles, from behind, in front and above the stage and even right beside him on a couple of times. He pounded for twenty minutes at a stretch displaying unyielding stamina and colossal technique. The solo always went down well and paved the way for *Whole Lotta Love*.

We took the train from Düsseldorf to Frankfurt glimpsing the Rhine, and later flew from Frankfurt to Berlin. In Frankfurt they played to 11,000 at the Festhall and here I managed to join in timbales during *Whole Lotta Love*, hammering at the drums with a pair of sticks and wondering if anybody could hear me. Gazing out at the cheering throng I got an idea of the emotions that seize the breast of every rock star facing his audience. I wanted to grab the microphone and order everyone to invade Poland.

They broke the attendance record of any rock group in Germany with their Frankfurt show which featured *The Immigrant Song, Heart Breaker, Dazed And Confused, Bring It On Home, That's The Way, Since I've Been Loving You* and *What Is And Should Never Be*, followed by *Moby Dick, Whole Lotta Love, Communication Breakdown* and their famed rock 'n' roll medley.

We went to Berlin on Sunday and visited the Berlin Wall which filled everyone with gloom and depression. Robert was particularly upset when I explained to him that West Berlin was completely surrounded by East German territory, although I wondered at the time what those grammar schools up in the Midlands were teaching in the way of modern history!

By now the heavy touring was taking its toll of their health and nerves. Jimmy was suffering from nausea and diarrhoea, Bonzo kept drawing blood on his hands and there was a general sense of fatigue. I asked Robert if he fancied a drink and an interview in the bar of the Berlin Hilton before the gig, and to my consternation he refused. He was ready to chat casually between gigs, but would not talk in depth about himself. I gathered it was nothing personal. He was trying to play down his starring role in the band.

In the meantime I kept my camera trained on the band at the Berlin concert and watched in amusement when Peter Grant busily put a stop to repeated attempts to make pirate recordings. These weren't fans but professionals armed with stereo mikes on boom stands. The disgruntled 'engineers' standing in front of the stage soon found their tapes being unceremoniously confiscated. Peter ripped one tape spool off the machine and began tearing it up. The German raged and rushed off to find a policeman, after Peter had pushed him out of the way with his stomach (possibly an old wrestlers' dodge). The policeman duly arrived, and took one look at Peter who glared ominously back. The policeman blanched and retreated shaking his head. He didn't want any aggravation.

The show at the Berlin Deutschlandhalle was tremendously exciting as the band hit a peak of performance. I went to a night club with the band afterwards, full of strange looking denizens of the twilight zone who could have been men or women, or both. Said John Bonham eyeing them with some concern. 'There's some weird looking people about.

75

There's nowhere for a decent bloke to have a pint of beer!'

I remember being so overcome with the exhaustion not to mention the German beer, wines and spirits that I wandered out of one such club intending to get a breath of fresh air and got lost wandering around a Kafka-esque townscape, full of dark and forbidding buildings that made Gothic architecture look modern. Eventually I found my way back to the Hilton where my night's sleep was disturbed by hideous howls. I discovered later that the reason for these noises was not some aberration of a fevered brain, but a tiger in the Berlin Zoo venting his protest at captivity and probably at the saxophone player with the dance band in the ballroom on the groundfloor.

After my tour of Germany with Led Zeppelin I was convinced that despite my sojourn on the timbales, I could never join the band. I just couldn't stand the pace!

SIX

STAIRWAY TO HEAVEN

By the end of 1970 Led Zeppelin had to take stock and recuperate. The feelings uppermost in their minds were that they needed to diversify their music and take a rest. They could not become automatons, just churning out riffs night after night on the road. There had to be time to think and to grow.

Said John Bonham: 'We are slackening off the pressure so we can work more in England. We played six nights a week for a month and I was doing my long drum solo every night. My hands were covered in blisters. We did six tours of America in fifteen months and the whole of the last tour was a sell-out.' This was their sixth US tour which had begun in Cincinatti on August 5, 1970 and while they were on the road they slotted in mixing sessions for their next album. They were already playing some of the songs from *Led Zeppelin III*, long before its October release.

After a break for a short holiday in Hawaii the tour ended on September 19 with two concerts at Madison Square Garden, New York where they grossed over one hundred thousand dollars. Back home the group were voted top in a Melody Maker poll and gold discs were presented to them by Anthony Grant, the Parliamentary Secretary to the Board of Trade. They were for selling more than a million copies of the *Led Zeppelin II* album in Europe. The Government recognised the band's efforts in helping exports and the balance of payments. Another gold disc came for advance orders for *Led Zeppelin III*.

While Peter Grant went to rest at a health farm to recover from all the touring, and to lose some weight, the band went into the new Island studios to start work on the next album. They moved on to Headley Grange, a house in Hampshire they used for rehearsing, and continued recording there using the Rolling Stones mobile studio.

By February 1971 the new album was virtually complete and they began the British tour that John Bonham had promised, in March. Known as the 'return of the clubs' tour, they played some of the small venues where they had started out, in a spirit of nostalgia and thanksgiving. The most dramatic dates on the tour were the two concerts they played in Ireland. The 'troubles' of Northern Ireland had been raging for two years and a visit by a leading pop group from mainland Britain, especially to Belfast, was regarded as daring and courageous, rather like ENSA entertainers going to the battle front during the Second World War.

These were the first UK concerts since the Bath Festival and the idea was to keep fees and ticket prices low. Despite the band's attempts to say 'thank you' to the fans, there were still grumbles, mainly from those who couldn't get into the packed venues.

Once again I accompanied the band, flying to Ireland with Melody Maker photographer Barrie Wentzell. The group were to play at the Ulster Hall, Belfast on March 5, and although I had been to Belfast before, there was nothing to compare with the drama and excitement of Zeppelin's concert. I'd been to Belfast with The Nice, for a concert featuring their brilliant organist Keith Emerson in 1968 and a few months later in July 1969 with The Nice, Yes and the Bonzo Dog Band. We saw the strange rumblings of discontent, long before they were being reported back in England; we noted the curious reaction when the Bonzo's saxophonist innocently played *Rule Britannia* in the street outside the Ulster Hall (passers-by growled warnings), and the bizarre practice in the villages we drove through, where every manhole, gutter pipe and telephone pole was painted red, white and blue. (We assumed they were having a village fete).

I particularly remembered the furtive, almost terrified air of the dignitaries we were introduced to on the 1968 trip with The Nice. I was with Keith Emerson, drummer Brian Davison and bassist Lee Jackson in the dressing room, sharing the delights of a handrolled cigarette which was being passed around, when suddenly a voice bellowed: 'Gentlemen – the Prime Minister!' In came the haggard looking leader who was asked to stand and pose with the group, who hastily concealed the still smouldering joint behind their backs. There was a strangely glazed and preoccupied look about all the faces in the subsequent photograph.

So I had strong impressions of Belfast before arriving there with Zeppelin, just before the real crisis began. It seemed to me the problems weren't caused so much by the well publicised conflict of religions, as a general malaise, a feeling of frustration and of being trapped in a drab environment. Feuding seemed like a welcome alternative to social imprisonment. It all reminded me of a childhood in war damaged London. In the East End we formed gangs to fight kids from the next street, for no other reason than they weren't from 'our street'. We built elaborate forts on bombsites, out of corrugated iron and hurled bricks and 'debris' at each other, or passing trains. It was exciting to risk danger and feel a sense of belonging to an elite group. My role in the Hamfrith Road gang ended when we were all taken home to our parents by the police. I was seven years old. The rest of the gang wasn't much older. Now the grown ups were forming gangs, and you couldn't just tick them off...

In a well meaning, if perhaps pompous way I tried to write about the Led Zeppelin concert in Belfast as a shining example of how youth could co-operate and be united – in a love for rock 'n' roll. And in point of fact the fans at the concert in the Ulster Hall were united, while outside on the streets, the gangs and the authorities were fighting the first battles of a conflict that is to go on, it seems, for ever. I reported in the Melody Maker: 'A new kind of riot hit Ireland last weekend. A riot of fun, laughter and excitement, when Led Zeppelin paid their first visit to the troubled isle. The Britons who brought guitars instead of guns were given an ecstatic welcome. Cheering fans in Belfast and Dublin knew no barriers when it came to appreciating the return of the world's greatest rock band.

'Zeppelin have been off duty for several months. But they tore into their new round of appearances with electrifying exuberance. Violence and explosions raged only half a mile away from their concert in Belfast on Friday night. But the young people of the town, unconcerned with ancient conflicts, used their energy to celebrate the worthwhile cause of peace, love and music.'

I hadn't entirely taken it on myself to propagate these worthy sentiments. Many local Belfast people had made a point of telling me that not everyone was involved in the feuding and that most just wanted to get on with their lives and leave other people alone. Zeppelin themselves perhaps wisely refrained from comments on the situation. Their presence and their music alone spoke volumes.

The band enjoyed the concerts hugely and Robert told me: 'We are all different personalities, but there is a kind of magic when we get together again.' The reaction was so favourable in Ireland they all said they wished they had gone there earlier. The Belfast fans in particular were delighted to see a group had visited them when so many English bands had chickened out of going to the trouble torn town. The night we arrived a petrol tanker was hijacked, a youth was shot dead and fire bombs were being hurled. Fortunately we didn't see much evidence of this on our journey from the airport to the Ulster Hall. We saw a lone British soldier in a keep and students from Queens University holding rag day festivities, throwing nothing more dangerous than flour bombs at passers by and parading the streets in warpaint.

We arrived at the hall for a soundcheck and then the fans came in; boys and girls who literally ran to their seats. The battering introduction to *Immigrant Song* shook the stage as the band started the historic concert. Robert Plant strutted around the small area between the towering speaker columns in a black and red blouse, smiling greetings through his mass of golden hair. On the flight over the band had complained of being 'rusty' after a lay off. But there were no signs of rust about their performance. THe sound was clean and free of distortion, and they seemed sparked by the crowd's enthusiasm as they played old favourites like *Heart Breaker, Since I've Been Loving You, Dazed And Confused* and *Whole Lotta Love*.

A storm of applause greeted *Since I've Been Loving You* with its slow, measured, grandiose introduction. Jimmy played beautifully fluent blues choruses, while John Bonham played some explosive breaks and fill-ins.

They played a lot of material from their fourth album including *Black Dog* a heavy rocker which was greeted with much cheering. Another new song was *Stairway To Heaven*, with Jimmy on double necked guitar, which gave him a twelve string and six string sound on the same instrument. I described it as an 'excellent ballad which displayed Robert's developing lyricism.' It was the first time *Stairway To Heaven* had been heard in public and I can remember asking Robert the title of the 'new ballad' as an afterthought. It was a moving song, but nobody then dreamed it would become such a classic and so closely identified with the band, particularly in America where it was played on radio for years – to this very day.

After the ovation which greeted *Stairway* and *Moby Dick* at Belfast, Robert told the audience: 'A lot of those musical papers that come from across the sea say we are going to break up. Well – WE'RE NEVER GOING TO BREAK UP!'

A roar went up and the band launched into their final numbers, *Boogie Mama* and *Communication Breakdown*. Fans rushed the stage as the house lights went up. 'If we could all be like this every minute of every day there would be no hang ups, no problems,' said Robert. For ten minutes the audience clamoured for more and just as a worried attendant was saying 'Please boys and girls – the concert is over,' Zeppelin returned, to play a few minutes more.

80

I talked to one of the fans outside their dressing room afterwards, a girl called Anita. 'Are they an English band? I always thought they came from America. I always thought Robert Plant was fat and Jimmy Page was tall from a picture I have at home. You get these funny notions.'

After the show the group and their manager drove in separate cars across the border to Dublin where we checked in at the Inter-Continental Hotel. John Bonham had his own car and actually drove through the Falls Road riot area by mistake.

'The street was covered in glass and there were armoured cars and kids chucking things,' he said later. 'We just kept our heads down and drove right through.' The rest of the party had stopped off at a ballroom near the border for a cup of tea. Here a show band was playing and crowds of suspicious youths glared at Zeppelin without recognising them. I heard that the ballroom was later blown up. And all further concerts in Belfast were cancelled.

An altogether more friendly and relaxed mood prevailed in Dublin where the band were to play at the Boxing Stadium. A new stage had to be constructed during the afternoon to accommodate all Zeppelin's equipment. The show was another triumph, although after the hysteria of Belfast it seemed a lot slower in catching fire. By the end of the evening, with Robert roaring into an improvised rock medley, Dublin responded with the same fervour. As a bonus they played *Summertime Blues*, with Atlantic Records executive Phil Carson, jamming on bass guitar. Phil had earlier played bass with Dusty Springfield's backing group, as he never tired of telling everyone. One night in Japan, the band invited Phil to sit in once again, on *Whole Lotta Love*. But when the curtain went up and the audience gazed expectantly, all they saw was Phil Carson, left entirely on his own in the middle of the stage clutching his bass, desperately attempting to play the riff by himself, and un-leashing an outbreak of Japanese booing.

Meanwhile, back in Ireland, the two concerts put the band in high spirits. I was sitting in the Inter-Continental Hotel lounge, when Robert made a grand entry, cartwheeling across the floor and a settee, much to the astonishment of the inevitable middle aged American tourists. Later that night, as a party spirit seized the band, words were ex-changed between Robert and Bonzo. Plant's habit of taking the mickey out of his old mate (he invariably presented him with a banana after each drum solo), was beginning to draw a heated response, and they came to blows. It was at three in the morning when there came a great hammering on a particular bedroom door in the hotel corridor. It was Bonzo sounding terribly guilty and upset: 'Peter – I've done a terrible thing. I've hit Robert!' Came the irritated response of a manager need-lessly roused from his slumbers, 'Shut up and go to bed!'

Tactfully nobody said anything about the early morning rumpus, as

81

our BEA Trident flew (just about) in a series of bumps across the Irish sea back to London the next day. 'I enjoyed Ireland and wish we could come back,' Jimmy Page told me, looking tired and ill. 'We're not playing the great long three hour shows now, but like to give a good balanced programme, with new and old material.'

Jimmy talked about the new songs and *Led Zeppelin IV*. 'On the LP John Paul Jones had over-tracked recorders on the introduction to *Stairway To Heaven* which we can't reproduce on stage, but the acoustic guitars come off okay. I still get a great kick out of playing our older numbers like *Dazed And Confused* and *The Immigrant Song*. The new LP is due out in April and might be called *Zeppelin IV*. Everybody expects that but we might change it. We've got all sorts of mad ideas. We were thinking at one time of putting out four EPS. But we want to keep the price down and frankly the price of records now is extortionate. The only way we can make up for it is by giving more playing time.

'And with this sort of music the whole thing is to get as much 'level' as you can, so the records sound as good on any kind of player. If the level is down you may lose a lot of basic sound. You have to check that in the cutting stage and quality control.'

I asked Jimmy if there was any particular theme or mood about the new album.

'Well *Stairway To Heaven* is a pretty good representation of what we are doing now. There are different moods in the song which lasts ten minutes. We want to do a really long track one day, but not yet. There is quite a lot of instrumental work as well. On our gigs we have been trying to cut down the volume. There are so many complaints about volume and people have been linking us with Grand Funk Railroad. I can't see ANY comparison! It really hurts to be compared to a band which is just about volume. We did acoustic things on our first album and I would have thought that created a precedent for us. I've never heard Grand Funk Railroad get into those kind of things.

'We know where we are going as a group. We are four individuals who have found a common denominator in music. There is a lot of inspiration coming through on this new album. We're getting better all the time. Robert's words to *Stairway To Heaven* are brilliant – the best Robert has ever written.'

Throughout March the band played universities and clubs in England climaxing with the Marquee Club, London on March 23. Peter Grant chuckled when he recalled the reaction of Jack Barrie, manager of the Marquee when he called up and said Zeppelin wanted to play at the club. They thought it was a hoax call!'

Jimmy Page explained the idea behind the tour. 'We were losing contact with people. By doing a tour this way we will re-establish contact with our audience and re-energise ourselves on the reaction.'

The public were becoming specks on the horizon at concerts. It made you feel you were looking through the wrong end of a telescope. In the clubs you are close enough to people to pick up on their reactions – you can see their faces.'

In July they played at the Vigorelli Stadium in Milan, Italy. When 12,000 fans stood up to applaud after a couple of numbers, police and soldiers over-reacted and attacked them with batons and tear gas. There was a riot and the group's equipment was stolen or damaged. At first the group thought the smoke was being caused by the crowd lighting fires. Then they realised it was police firing tear gas cannisters, and some of the gas began drifting onto the stage. The band were surrounded by people milling around the backstage area, as well as out front, and feared being trapped. They played one more number followed by *Whole Lotta Love* and then the crowd jumped onto the stage. Someone threw a bottle at the police who had been goading them with the tear gas, and the riot began.

The band escaped through a tunnel filled with gas, and locked themselves into their dressing room. Outside the road crew raced around trying to salvage the equipment, and several had to be carried off on stretchers.

The band also suffered from problems with the new album which had been mixed in California – badly. The whole lot had to be remixed before the album could be released on November 8 – without a proper title. There had been much argument about the name, and *Led Zeppelin IV* seemed a bit of a cop-out. It was decided to choose a different symbol for each member of the band which represented their characters and this was featured on the inner sleeve.

Jimmy Page was represented by the mysterious phrase 'Zoso', John Paul Jones by intertwined ovals, John Bonham by three sturdy linked rings, and Robert Plant by a feather inside a circle. The cover showed a portrait of an old man bearing a huge bundle of rods and bent under the weight, while the back cover shot showed a photograph of slum clearance and high rise developments. Inside the gatefold sleeve was what looked like a charcoal drawing of another old man, this time holding a lantern and a stick, perched on top of a mountain overlooking a distant castle. It was called 'The Hermit' and was done by artist Barrington Colby. There was no other information visible on the sleeve, about group or record company. It was described by worried executives as 'commercial suicide'. And for most bands, it would have been.

Jimmy explained the meaning behind the artwork: 'The old man on the cover, carrying the wood is in harmony with nature. He takes from nature and gives back to the land. It's a natural circle – it's right. His old cottage gets pulled down and they put him in these urban slums – old slums, terrible places. The old man is also the Hermit of the Tarot cards –

83

a symbol of self-reliance and mystical wisdom.'

The tracks included *Black Dog, Rock And Roll, The Battle Of Evermore, Stairway To Heaven, Misty Mountain Hop, Four Sticks, Going To California* and *When The Levee Breaks*.

In August the band played twenty concerts on their seventh tour of America, earning a million dollars in the process. They played five shows in Japan in October including a charity show for victims of Hiroshima. The band's off-stage mayhem during this tour earned them reputations as ravers throughout Japan, and the Hilton Hotel in Tokyo banned them for life.

To coincide with the release of the album, the group began their second British tour of the year, starting at Newcastle City Hall on November 11. They played two shows at the Empire Pool, Wembley on November 20 and 21 and 19,000 tickets for the shows sold out in an hour. The price of tickets, in those pre-inflationary times, was just 75p. The band was supported by Bronco and Stone The Crows and a whole bunch of circus acts.

The tour finished in Bournemouth on December 2 and the group released a single – *Black Dog* – in America which got to Number Fifteen in the charts. They refused to release *Stairway To Heaven* as a single however, and none were released in England. All the world – except Singapore which banned them for wearing long hair – wanted to see Led Zeppelin. And so British fans were deprived of any view of the band for many months ahead. Most of 1972 was spent touring in Australia, New Zealand (where they played to 25,000 people in Auckland), America and Japan. They were playing three hour shows night after night, but had to cut back on some of the songs, or risk total exhaustion.

At last British fans were rewarded when the group played an extensive tour starting on November 30 at Newcastle City Hall. They played eighteen cities and sold out all the tickets in a day. The dates continued into 1973 followed by a European tour in March.

The fifth Led Zeppelin album *Houses Of The Holy* was released in March, several months behind schedule because of work problems. Advance orders were colossal and it went gold in Germany alone before it was even released. Robert Plant discussed the new album and said: 'All our albums are different and in four years we have covered all sorts of ground. We have a track called *The Crunge* which is really funny, something we would never have imagined us doing. We've also written a reggae number which I would like out as a single.'

I reviewed the album and thought that it wasn't up to standard. I didn't like either *The Crunge* or the reggae number, and said so, not realising I was treading on Robert's toes as the man behind these new directions in Zeppelin music. Despite mixed reviews the album went straight to Number One and *D'Yer Mak'er* was released as a single in America where it scraped into the charts.

On their next thirty-three date tour of America the band used a Boeing 720B jet airliner to get to gigs, and earned nearly five million dollars. It began in Atlanta and after they played a show in front of 50,000 the mayor said it was, 'the biggest thing to hit Atlanta since *Gone With The Wind.*' Shouted Robert Plant to the fans: 'Do you feel it, do you feel the buzz?' By now the group were at the forefront of the big league concert attractions of the early Seventies, with a crew of thirty and tons of equipment for the light show and sound system.

The shows were a symphony of music, strobe lights, smoke and spinning mirrors. The Showco company of Dallas, Texas excelled themselves in providing the best possible setting for Zeppelin's music. If the band had been upset by my review of *Houses Of The Holy* then there were plenty of compensations. They earned nearly 250,000 dollars for the Atlantic Braves Stadium show and when they played at Tampa, Florida, they broke another record, the one held by the Beatles since 1965 when they attracted 55,000 to the Shea Stadium. Zeppelin drew 56,800. It was important that all this history making be preserved. Work began on a major film, the smash hit movie *The Song Remains The Same* which was also the title of a song on *Houses Of The Holy.*

Other tracks on the album included *The Rain Song, Over The Hills And Far Away, The Crunge, Dancing Days, D'yer Mak'er, No Quarter* and *The Ocean.* It was recorded at Electric Lady Studios in New York and Olympic in London. The cover depicted naked girls climbing up some rocks.

Filming was by director Joe Massott and he started work on July 18, taking his cameras to gigs at Baltimore, Boston, Pittsburgh and New York's Madison Square Garden on July 28. Joe was a friend of Jimmy Page's girlfriend, Charlotte and his idea was to represent each member of the group and introduce them into the structure of the film. He wanted to avoid *Woodstock* style documentary, although in retrospect a proper documentary by a major TV network would have been more interesting.

The band played three nights at Madison Square – July 27, 28 and 29. It was after the second night that the group's tour manager, Richard Cole, and attorney Steve Weiss put two hundred thousand dollars into a safe deposit box at the Drake hotel. This was intended to cover expenses and wages. But the money went missing from the box. The group heard the news during Bonzo's *Moby Dick* solo. After a party where gold discs were presented the group went back to the hotel where press and TV crews arrived to interview the group. But they refused to talk about the alleged robbery. In the ensuing row Peter Grant was arrested for hitting a photographer who was pestering him. Richard Cole had to take a lie detector test, and was subsequently cleared of being involved.

It was an extraordinary business, and marked the turning point in Zeppelin's good relations with media at large. From here on the group began to be dogged with bad luck, misfortune and unwelcome publicity. The group left America, having offered a ten thousand dollar reward for information about the robbery, but there was never anymore said about the mystery and the money was never found. Jimmy had been ill during the tour and sprained a finger which affected his playing. On return to England he announced he wanted 'a nice long sleep'.

He added: 'I expect we'll start work on a new album. It seems so long since we had a break. I can't remember when we were not working. It's been an incredible tour, but we're all terribly worn out. I went past the point of no return physically quite a while back but now I've gone past the mental point. I've only kept going by functioning automatically.'

In September Robert Plant was voted Number One male singer in the Melody Maker poll and the band started work on the next album at Plumpton Manor, an eighteenth century residence, complete with fifty acres and lakes, which Jimmy had bought as his new home. He also owned Bokeskin House on the shores of Loch Ness which had once belonged to 'The Beast' Aleister Crowley. Sequences for the film *The Song Remains The Same*, featuring Jimmy as 'The Hermit' climbing rocks, were shot around the house and nearby mountains. For similar 'personality' sequences, Robert was filmed in the countryside and on the farm, while John Bonham had himself filmed driving a drag racing car on the American Santa Pod track.

Jimmy's segment was shot on the night of a full moon and involved special lighting with arc lamps and scaffolding erected on the mountain side.

Towards the end of 1973 Jimmy Page worked on recording some tracks for singer Maggie Bell, and also wrote some music for the soundtrack of a movie by underground director Kenneth Anger, called *Lucifer Rising*. Anger was an actor and film maker who shared Jimmy's interest in the occult, and Aleister Crowley.

The main event of 1974 was the decision by the band to increase their range of activities by forming their own record company called Swan Song, which would be distributed by Atlantic Records. Other groups had tried to form their own labels without much success, but Swan Song did eventually release worthwhile product by other groups including Maggie Bell, The Pretty Things and Bad Company. Led Zeppelin's own contract with Atlantic had just expired and their future product was issued on the Swan Song label but still distributed through Atlantic.

The Swan Song offices were set up above a British Legion headquarters in London's New Kings Road, a strangely low key affair, notable for its cheap furnishings, and dusty, cobwebbed appearance. Another office was set up in New York. Two launch parties were held, one at the Four Seasons restaurant in New York which cost ten thousand dollars and another in Los Angeles. Among suggested titles for the new label were Slut, Slag, Eclipse, De Luxe, Stairway and Zeppelin Records. The name Swan Song was chosen after Jimmy Page had originally suggested it for an acoustic guitar track. The name was later switched to an LP title and finally hived off to use for the label.

In October 1974 a party was held in Chislehurst Caves, Kent to celebrate the release of *Silk Torpedo* by the Pretty Things on the new label. There was much boozing and merriment, with entertainment provided by fire eaters and semi-naked wenches in the tradition of the Hell Fire caves. All who attended the party were speechless for days afterwards.

Despite these celebrations, and various jam sessions with Bad Company and Roy Harper, it was a strangely unproductive year as far as the group were concerned. Said Jimmy Page: '1974 didn't really happen. 1975 will be better.'

SEVEN

STRANGE DAYS

For British fans, 1975 stood out as the year of Earls Court. Zeppelin played five nights at the massive London exhibition centre on May 17,18,23,24 and 25, presenting their full American tour production. It was the first time many had ever seen the band, as a new generation, too young to hang out at the Marquee in the early days, discovered the now legendary 'super group'. They were privileged to see Zeppelin at their best. And although the group were forever grumbling in America that they got a bad press at home, in fact they received unanimously ecstatic reviews, both for the concerts and their new album *Physical Graffiti*.

America also went wild over the band who went on a tour while sales of the album soared. Yet it had looked as if the year might have to be virtually cancelled, not long after Jimmy Page had promised it would make up for the non-events of 1974.

Work commenced with two warm-up shows – Rotterdam, Holland on January 11 and Brussels, Belgium, the following day. The first shows in over a year, they were planned to help the band get into shape for the American tour, their tenth, due to start in Minneapolis on January 18.

Then came what might have been disaster. Jimmy Page, visiting London for rehearsals, caught his 'ring' finger in a train door at Victoria Station. At first it was thought he wouldn't be able to play for months, but after treatment it was agreed the show must go on. The band dropped *Dazed And Confused* from a few of their dates, to reduce the strain on Page's finger picking guitar work. They played the simpler *How Many More Times* instead.

It was just as well they decided to carry on. The tour was massive, even by Zeppelin standards, and caused mayhem as excitement over their visit built up. With their reputation at an all-time high, everyone from starry-eyed fans of *Stairway To Heaven* to crazed pill poppers and heavy metal freaks wanted to share the Zeppelin experience.

After fans rioted and smashed up a ticket office, the group were banned from playing one of their favourite cities – Boston – where they had first broken through back in the Sixties. Police had to control crowds desperate for tickets in most of the twenty-six cities they played and in all some 700,000 tickets were sold, usually all gone in a matter of hours. Zeppelin now had their stage act to a peak of technical perfection.

Although they had always been at heart a basic four piece rock band without any frills, they saw no reason not to invest their profits in making their show as visually exciting as new technology allowed. They used a 70,000 watt PA system and a 310,000 watt lighting rig and mirrors. They used the new technology of lasers, the first time the public were able to see the new wonder beams in action outside the realms of James Bond movies. Fans flinched when the beams passed over their bodies, expecting to be burned or vaporised.

The group hired the famed Starship, scene of much in-flight entertainment and escapades, to fly around the country, using the Butler Aviation hangar at Newark Airport as their base, and staying in a limited number of hotels. This was designed to reduce the number of disorientating stop-overs. There was no doubt the band were under a considerable strain. To the outsider it seemed a tremendously glamorous existence, and so it was, in small doses. Those who joined the tour for a few nights, perhaps as reporters, technicians or just friends, could be impressed by the statistics and the power and wealth generated by the band. But it took a toll on the nerves and health of the young musicians whose whole lives had been, in a sense, directed towards this goal of success in America.

The nightly succession of musical 'highs', the need to live up to expectations, the constant stream of strange faces, friends or foes, and living out of a suitcase was enough to unhinge anybody.

John Bonham began stuffing ice cubes and ferns from a hotel display inside the shirt of a bewildered young reporter who he decided was not only physically ugly but represented the ugly face of rock criticism. Jimmy Page admitted that he was close to a nervous and physical breakdown, while on a less dramatic level there were minor aches, pains and ailments to contend with.

Robert Plant went down with a bout of flu and a show in St. Louis had

89

to be cancelled. In Greensboro, North Carolina, there was more rioting, this time between police and fans trying to get tickets. After the show the band made a quick getaway with Peter Grant driving one of the cars at speeds up to seventy mph, with a police escort. Over a two month period the band grossed around five million dollars. Six concerts in the New York area alone resulted in 120,000 tickets selling out in thirty-six hours. The shows were at Madison Square Garden and Nassau Colosseum, Long Island, during February.

All the reigning rock stars turned out to greet the heroes of the hour. Mick Jagger and David Bowie went to see them play at Madison Square Garden, while Ron Wood and Rod Stewart went to the Long Island concert. John Lennon announced that he had heard *Stairway To Heaven* and approved. Robert was astonished. 'What – has he only just heard it?'

Top rock critic and Zeppelin fan, Lisa Robinson wrote: 'It's not that hard to understand why so many people are turned on by this four man British group who have consistently ravaged this country when they come here to tour, as well as outselling anyone else who attempts to get on the charts when Zep has a new LP out. They simply have their own kind of magic.'

America's gossip columnists went crazy over Zeppelin, seizing on every escapade and snippet of scandal about the band. But they remained tight lipped, evasive or simply laughed off most of the suggestions made about them. Occasionally under questioning they would admit, well yes Jimmy did enjoy the company of girls, and Bonzo did get a bit out of hand after a few drinks. What fascinated people most was the story of the mudsharks and Jimmy's interest in the occult. Richard Cole, their tour manager did once tell me in full detail the story of the mudshark escapade involving various 'nubiles'. Fins had been inserted into various orifices under the watchful eye of Bonzo. Frank Zappa was so taken with the story, he devoted a whole song to it, but Peter Grant told the best story – how they once concealed a mass of the finny creatures in a hotel bedroom cupboard, which fell out on an unsuspecting maid.

Undoubtedly Richard was master of Zeppelin revels or instigator of many of their exploits, carried out in cahouts with Bonzo and observed with giggles by the rest of the band. Pranks were played, practical jokes planned and vengeance wreaked. It wasn't only coincidence that Richard had earlier been a close associate of Keith Moon.

Richard, born 1945, started out as a 'roadie' working for such bands as Unit Four Plus Two, The Searchers, The New Vaudeville Band, The Who, The Yardbirds, Jeff Beck, Vanilla Fudge and The Rascals. He started with Zeppelin on their first gig on Boxing Day 1968. It was his job to drive the band, make travel arrangements, check flights, and look

after the boys. Warding off over persistent fans was one of his speciali-
ties. A strange man who could combine charm and friendship with
hovering, hidden menace, he could scare and intimidate people more
with a look and a gesture, than all the blustering others might adopt.

On one occasion a British national newspaper reporter was trying to
gain access to Zeppelin's dressing room and was barred by Richard on
the not unreasonable grounds that they were having a meeting. The
reporter took umbrage and felt slighted. He launched into the old tirade
of how he would ruin them and the band 'would never work again'. The
cool response was that the reporter would 'never walk again'.

The fans Cole dealt with more gently, giving free tickets to those who
fought their way backstage and begged for a chance to see their heroes.
Many were struck by the surprisingly small entourage that surrounded
Zeppelin on the road. With Grant and Cole, there was hardly need for
anybody else around. Although they cultivated a tough, underworld
image and took no nonsense, from the highest to the lowest, they were a
complex pair that few really understood. Jimmy Page insisted that Peter
was a gentle man despite the fierceness he showed to anyone who
might try to put one over his band. Said Peter: 'If you can survive in this
line of business then you can survive the jungle. I know I'm a mixed
character. But it's horses for courses isn't it? If someone's being rough
with you, you gotta be rough back. What makes me really angry is
people who let you down.'

If there was a dark side to Zeppelin they swiftly counteracted it with
their sense of humour and normal good nature. Once Lisa Robinson
asked John Bonham about the strange electronic noises he was producing during his *Moby Dick* drum solo.

'It's all magic,' he explained. 'Didn't you see me playing with me little
black wand?'

Even Robert's image as a sex symbol was the subject of much band
humour. After one outburst of outrageous camping, mincing, pouting
and strutting on stage in Detroit Peter Grant laughed: 'I keep telling him
he'll be ready for Las Vegas soon. I said to him "Percy – I've got Vegas
lined up for you."'

There were parties galore; but most of the time the band liked to get
away from the crush of visiting stars and hangers-on. Midway through
the tour Robert and Jimmy fled to the island of Dominique for a few
days, while Bonzo and John Paul went back to England to rest. Back in
California for the rest of the dates, Robert stayed in Malibu where he
could ride horses and swim before rejoining the band at the famed
Continental Hyatt House on Hollywood's Sunset Strip, also known as
the 'Riot House'. It was here Bonzo took to riding a motorcycle up and
down the corridors. The band wasn't so much into mindless destruc-
tion, although Bonzo was known to break the odd radio or TV set when

91

it 'wouldn't work'. They were more concerned with breaking up the boredom of the touring routine with creative play.

One man able to observe the full force of Zeppelin at work and play was their long suffering PR man, Bill Harry. A Liverpudlian, he founded and edited Merseybeat and was an early friend and champion of The Beatles. Bill came to London during the mid-Sixties and set up business as a publicity consultant.

A likeable man, he tended to have a hangdog look, doubtless the result of keeping close company with volatiles like John Lennon and John Bonham. He became the butt of endless pranks and practical jokes, which he usually endured with a stoical grin. He and his wife Virginia became showbiz celebrities in their own right, as they patrolled the night clubs of the world, ordering pints of lager and meat pies. Virginia was heard to announce in an exotic, cosmopolitan restaurant in the South of France, during a jazz festival, 'Ee, I could do with a nice cup of tea, and a bun.'

Bill had got to know Peter Grant several years before the formation of Led Zeppelin. Recalled Bill: 'What I liked about the Sixties was they were far more informal times. Everyone who was in the music business met for drinks, got on together socially and saw each other at gigs. I'd known Peter Grant from my days in Liverpool when I was running Merseybeat magazine and he was Gene Vincent's road manager. He had come to Liverpool when Gene played at the Locarno. I got to know and like him.'

In London Bill quickly found success as a PR. Anyone coming from Liverpool was then regarded as having a Midas touch. Among his clients were The Kinks, The Hollies and Pink Floyd. He remembers taking the Floyd on a trip to the BBC Radiophonic Workshop, where they were fascinated by the possibilities of electronic sound.

One of the rising rock agencies of the time was run by Terry Ellis and Chris Wright, whose organisation, from poor beginnings, without any money and few acts, grew into the mighty Chrysalis company. The original Ellis Wright agency asked Bill to take over Jethro Tull, Chicken Shack (with the ebullient Stan Webb on guitar), and Savoy Brown. The agency had moved into a small office in Oxford Street, London, and Bill rented a room in the same building to run his press and PR business. On the floors above Bill were Chrysalis , Island Music and then at the top, Peter Grant and Micky Most sharing an office.

As neighbours Micky Most asked Bill to handle press for his up and coming singer Terry Reid. Then when Peter Grant launched Led Zeppelin, he too called on Bill for assistance. But he soon found that 'doing the press' for Zeppelin would not be like any other account. For a start, they didn't really want to do any interviews ... and there weren't many papers who wanted to speak to them. It was no wonder Bill developed his lugubrious expression of amused resignation.

'They called Zeppelin an underground group because the national press didn't want to know about them. Nobody ever wrote about them or the other underground groups apart from International Times. I had a battle to get them established in the national music press. With Zeppelin it was different because they really didn't *want* press. They would only okay certain things. Jimmy would only want to talk to International Times (then the hippies' bible). And they wouldn't put out any singles either.'

Bill could see at first hand the curious policy that Zeppelin had adopted right from the beginning. 'They didn't want to take the conventional path to success like everybody else.'

Bill went to all their early gigs, from pubs to the Marquee Club, and didn't see any irony in the situation of being a PR for a band who didn't want PR. 'They had to have somebody doing the press, only because they got so many inquiries later on. I'd talk to them and say "Do you want to see so-and-so?" . . . and they'd say no! They didn't really want to know the press. They didn't want to do interviews. It was very difficult for me. All I could do was make a list of people who wanted interviews, and they just turned them down.

'The reason was they felt the press wasn't entirely honest. They were conscious of the press building artists up and then knocking them down. They decided not to have singles out and everyone told them it was suicide. The were told from the start if they didn't release singles, they would never be big. But they thought: "We, Led Zeppelin can exist without the press. We will not have the press saying we made you, and we're gonna knock you down. We can exist because the people who come to see us support our music and we're not having these people outside claiming to have built us up and then trying to knock us down." They were trying to distance themselves from the press. Eventually of course they did do interviews, when they got to know and like certain people, like Roy Carr of the NME. But they were aware how fickle and dishonest the press could be.'

One incident that aroused Zeppelin's suspicions was when a reporter from Record Mirror supposedly reviewing a Chicken Shack gig was taken tired and emotional after a long session in the band's hospitality room. He missed the gig when he passed out in the tent, and later rang Bill Harry demanding to know the set list of tunes performed. He wrote his review from the information supplied, and slagged off the band, proclaiming them awful.

Said Bill Harry: 'This happened regularly. I'd be at Led Zeppelin gigs which were phenomenal and the people went berserk, demanding four encores. The atmosphere would be magic. Then I'd read in the paper "Oh, they went down like a damp squib." I couldn't believe it. What

93

were they trying to do? I could understand different opinions about music, but when they distorted the facts, I could understand Zeppelin's attitude. And that happened a lot.

'I was with Zeppelin for four years. I travelled on the Continent with them and to America. It was most exciting because I'd done the same thing with The Beatles, as they grew from tiny cellar clubs in Liverpool, even before The Cavern, to play on the biggest stages in the world.

'It was the same story with Zeppelin and their shows were such mind blowers. Really they were a great bunch of lads into having a good time. It was a period of time when everything was extraordinary. They were superstars. But really they were just ordinary people under a lot of pressure which meant they led an extraordinary life, all the time. People wouldn't really allow them to be ordinary.

'To me, they came closer than any other group, including The Rolling Stones, to The Beatles. But they never reached their peak. They got big, but they could have been bigger. They had started to back pedal even before John Bonham's death. They turned down so many offers.

'And still the money just POURED in. Unbelievable. They were getting over twenty million pounds a year by the start of the Seventies. The American break through made them all millionaires within the year. They were so much bigger than The Rolling Stones in terms of money and the way people reacted to them. If there was a choice, Zeppelin was the band people wanted to see. If promoters were offered The Stones or Zeppelin, they'd take Zeppelin.

'Now it seems people have forgotten how big they were. People's memories are short. It was absolutely amazing what they achieved in a relatively short time. And they could have achieved even more. They had the brakes on all the time. Just as they wouldn't release singles, they limited everything else.'

Bill believed there was a master plan behind Zeppelin's success. 'They all sat down and talked and decided what *they* wanted to do. They wouldn't waiver. They would determine their own destiny and not let it be determined by outside forces. The whole system, of record companies and promoters, could have taken them over. They could have been made to work 365 days of the year, seven days a week, and they would have burned themselves out, under pressure to make more and more records. They could have spent all their time doing interviews, and nothing else.'

Bill confirms that many attempts were made to rip off Zeppelin, but no single predator had tried to take over the band, as happened with the Beatles and Stones. 'No. Peter Grant had an aura about him and people were frightened of him. But Peter Grant was a great guy, I never found him once threatening. He was quite considerate with people. But he was very tough and had a protective thing about Zeppelin.

94

'He knew the business inside out and knew there were so many attempts to con them. Money was stolen from them all the time. The ticket money from a show would be lodged in a safe, and then after a gig, the safe would be 'robbed', and there was no money. But he knew the promoters were trying to con him. He knew what the 'gates' were and he wanted the money straight away. He'd tell the promoter how much had been earned. He HAD to be tough or else he'd be stitched up, and somebody else would make all the money for their efforts.

'He was aware of all this from his experience as a roadie. He'd seen how Gene Vincent had been conned wicked. Gene was ripped off like nobody's business, and Peter Grant knew this. And he was making sure it didn't happen to Zeppelin. That's why he got a heavy reputation. All he wanted was the money that was due to them. Because he wouldn't let people backstage during a show – hangers on and groupies – they would go away and grumble that Peter was a 'heavy'. But legitimate guests would always be allowed back.'

How did Peter fend off the 'heavies' in America who wanted a piece of the action? 'Sheer presence. You could tell by looking at him "This guy is serious. He's not kidding!" He had this fantastically powerful presence, but he was just a friendly warm guy. I really liked him. But he had to be tough on the business side. He wasn't interested in screwing people like some rock managers. But he made sure he wasn't screwed. Nobody messed around with Peter. The word was play fair with him and he'd play fair with you. That's why he got on great with the promoters.'

But things did go sour, later on, notably in the punch up incident between the Zeppelin crew and men working for promoter Bill Graham. How did Bill explain this aberration?

'If there was a fight, there must have been provocation because normally they just weren't like that. I wasn't around then, I had left, so I don't know. But there were always cops and security guards and detectives on the make. Palms were greased.'

Bill had seen this method of oiling the Zeppelin machine early in their conquest of America. They had gone to play the famous Newport Jazz Festival on July 6, 1969. At the hotel Bill was robbed of his wallet, credit cards and all his money. He was left penniless and stranded, because the group had not yet arrived in the country. 'I didn't have a cent, and I was in an alien country, staying at one of the most expensive hotels in Newport. I was praying the group would turn up and rescue me. Then I heard on the radio that Led Zeppelin had been told they couldn't appear at the festival because all the roads from Boston were blocked by thousands of kids coming in to see Zeppelin. The police and the authorities didn't want them for fear of riots. I was very worried.

'Then I got a call from Peter Grant to say "We're on our way". The rumours had been put out to try and stop the fans from coming, because there were already a couple of hundred thousand people on the hills around the festival site. The streets were blocked and the freeways were jammed with cars for miles. Newport was a small town and couldn't cope with such an influx. It seemed the entire population of under thirty-year-olds of Boston had arrived.

'After the concert there was a party. George Wein the promoter invited us and there were all the famous names of jazz, like Buddy Rich and Nina Simone. There were polite speeches and applause.'

None of this appealed to Zeppelin, panting from the excitement of the show. The boys began knocking back lagers and joined in a loud chorus of the Danny & The Juniors hit, *At The Hop*. The guests stared in some dismay, especially when Richard Cole and John Bonham got up on the table and started dancing, only to collapse into a heap.

The jazz celebrities hurriedly vacated the room and the party was over. John was most upset. 'Why are they all going? We've only just started' The group filled sacks with cans of lager and went back to their rooms with various lady guests. They were trailed by the house detective who warned them that guests weren't allowed in the rooms. Richard gave the detective twenty dollars and the house rules were suddenly relaxed.

In New York one of the entourage took Bonham's trousers off while he was playing drums on stage. Cops came and grabbed Bonzo and threatened to jail him for indecent exposure. They were paid three hundred dollars and the show went on with no charges made.

'This was America. The cops and security guards regarded it as perks. The bribes were like paying taxes. After all the guys were earning tens of thousands of dollars. But the Americans admired people who made a lot of money and the attitude was "Good luck to them".'

Despite all the money that poured in, the band themselves hardly ever carried any cash. They became adept at passing bills on to others, thinking that eventually the bill would come back to the band. Said Bill: 'They never spent any money while I was with them! I heard about Jimmy buying houses, but they never had any money to spend. If they were in a restaurant, they would order champagne and send the bill over to Phil Carson from Atlantic. The same thing would happen to me. I'd go down to the Speakeasy Club in London and the waiter would say: "Mr. Bonham has seen you arrive and sends you his bill." I'd say: "Get stuffed!" I'd learnt by then.'

Bill recalled that Jimmy Page became known as 'Led Wallet' because of his alleged careful attitude. 'There was a story that he came into town one day with a certain amount of money allocated for buying Christmas presents. He spent it all and then hitch hiked home. That's how he got the reputation. The fact is they just didn't bother to carry any money

Previous page: **Victory and peace . . .
Percy points the way**
Above: **Meet the brightest hopes for
1968**
Top right: **Butter wouldn't melt . . .**
Right: **Zeppelin with strings, but no
music**

Left: **Zeppelin blast songs from** *Four Symbols* **in 1971**
Top: **John Paul Jones ponders The Meaning Of Life**
Above: **Bonzo with tymps and gong**

Top left: **Robert at Swansong's notorious Chislehurst caves party with U.S. rock writer, Lisa Robinson**
Bottom left: **Jimmy Page entertains at the Pangbourne boat house, February 1970**
Above: **Peter Grant (centre) with MM writer Roy Hollingworth and the boys in Paris**
Right: **Happy Jim beside the Thames on a winter day in 1970**

Above: **Zeppelin triumph at the Bath Festival, June 1970**
Right: **Peter Grant, family man, with daughter Helen**
Bottom right: **Robert jams with his old mates Dave Edmunds and Nick Lowe**
Top right: **Paul McCartney, Peter Townshend and Robert at the 1979 'Rockestra' sessions**
Next page: **Plant out on the tiles with his own band in 1983**

around.

'They stopped in a record shop in Amsterdam and saw a great Jimi Hendrix LP. Up went the cry – "Pay for it Bill". They assumed I added it on to my bill, but I never did.'

Despite their fame and riches, Zeppelin were not always accorded royal treatment. The outside world was often hostile and threatening towards the strange party of long haired young men. And attitudes were much more conservative outside of America, in the so-called progressive countries.

Said Bill: 'I remember going to Sweden with them and they were booked into a nice hotel. But they wouldn't let them in because of their long hair. This was in 1970. We were right in the centre of town, close to the gig, and they wouldn't allow us in. We were told to go to another hotel out of town. They wouldn't let us in there either. We ended up in a third hotel, and then we were only allowed in if we went straight to the rooms and stayed there. We couldn't eat in the restaurant or mix with the people.'

The same thing happened to the band in Amsterdam. They were refused admission to the Americana hotel, and despatched to another hotel out among the windmills. By the time they had sorted out accommodation it was time to go back to the city centre for the concert. Then they had to find a place to eat and the restaurant wouldn't serve them. Everything they ordered on the menu they were told was 'off'. They had enough money to buy the restaurant, but they couldn't sit down for a meal. Eventually they had to send out for sandwiches.

Such hassles inevitably encouraged a contempt within the band for hotels, which became not the sort of luxurious palaces their parents might have dreamed about staying in, but prisons. The combination of frustration, money, high spirits and the need for release had predictable results.

'Like the Beatles, Led Zeppelin lived in a closed world,' recalled Bill Harry. 'I used to go to gigs with John Lennon and we'd go to a pub afterwards, but it got to the stage where The Beatles couldn't go out and they'd be sitting locked in a room all day. That can be intensely boring. John would say "I'd give anything just to be able to go down to the pub and have a drink."

'Travelling with Zep was just the same. Always hotel rooms... staying in all day waiting for the gig. It's not so glamorous. Groups going around the world found they were going from one prison to the next. It was a form of protest when they started going a bit mad. It was all practical jokes to them, but it could get on your nerves at times, particularly if you were with a band that was earning a lot of money, and you were not. They could cause damage and get away with it, and pay for it, but if your suit was ruined in the process it was a terrible bore.

97

'It happened to me many times. I'd go into the Speakeasy wearing a nice new suit and suddenly a plate of spaghetti came sailing through the air. I could see it was funny from their point of view, but not for me, not with spaghetti all over me clothes.'

All Bill had to do was send an invoice for the cleaning costs, but he never did. He just had to grin and bear it. The main spaghetti throwers were Bonzo, Plant and Cole. John Paul Jones remained a perfect gentleman, while Jimmy rarely joined in such pranks.

Bonzo was undoubtedly the most rumbustious, and learnt his lessons in the art of practical joking from Richard Cole and Keith Moon, with encouragement from drinking partner Stan Webb. Often Bill was the butt of his jokes, unless he saw the warning signals and fled in time. Horseplay had been a feature of his terms of employment right from the beginning and he took some grim satisfaction when others were the victims. 'I heard they were going to pay these groupies to strip Chris Welch naked. That's the plan they had for you.'

Often Bill was simply asked to make sure there was an endless flow of drinks. When they were having a party in a New York hotel, there was imminent danger of running out of spirits. Bill was despatched to find a bottle of Scotch. The hotel desk clerk, pointing out it was 2am, said there was no way a bottle could be provided. 'Forget it, go to bed,' was his advice. Said Bill: 'You must be joking.' He went outside the hotel, knocked on a promising looking door, explained he was from Led Zeppelin who were having a party, and a bottle of Scotch was given free, just for the honour of supplying the band. A couple of minutes later Bill walked back into the hotel, triumphantly waved his prize at the disbelieving receptionist.

Another night Bonzo demanded Bill accompany him to The Revolution, one of London's popular music business clubs. It was five minutes to three in the morning and the bar was about to close. Bill reckoned they only had time for one drink. Bonzo strode up to the bar and ordered fifty lagers, duly delivered to the table.

But it was the parties in America, away from the prying eyes of the press, where the group had most fun. 'We went to all the clubs in America, and the places were flooded with groupies. And all the time I was with Led Zeppelin I never once saw drugs being used. It was always booze and mainly lager. Everybody had hangovers. But most of it was caused through the stress of sitting around for hours in rooms before a gig. It was mind numbing. There'd be nothing to do so there was fifteen hours of tension before a gig.'

Drinking and partying was a funny way to fill in the time, although it would play havoc with their nerves and health. Bill recalled one party after a concert at the Winterland in San Francisco. The promoter, Bill Graham was delighted by their tremendously successful performance

98

and decided to throw a big party in their honour. The Winterland didn't have proper facilities so he hired a suite at a nearby hotel. After the show they went to the suite. Suddenly the doors opened and two trolleys came in, bearing naked girls with the food placed over their bodies.

'Bill Graham gave everybody foam cream to spray over the girls. The drinks were flowing and there were all kinds of orgies going on with people taking polaroid pictures. Somebody was having it off with a girl in a bath while pictures were taken. But I don't think it was one of the group. They had all gone back to the hotel. But Screaming Lord Sutch (the eccentric British rock 'n' roller) had joined the party. He soon conked out on the bed and was the only one left.

'But whoever had been having the bath had left the taps on and the water started going over the carpets. After a couple of hours it leaked through the ceiling and somebody complained to the manager.

'The manager and house detective started banging on the door, then used the pass key to get into the sodden bedroom. They found Lord Sutch lying on the bed, covered in polaroid photos of all the action.'

One of the most famous 'lost afternoons' began one lunch time in the more prosaic setting of the Coach & Horses pub in Poland Street, Soho, back in London. It was here that John Bonham frequently presided over a gathering of roadies and special guest star boozers, like Stan Webb and Glen Cornick, bass player with Jethro Tull. This particular team began drinking a special concoction of Vodka and Scotch which cost £1.50 a glass – a considerable sum in pre-inflationary times. Bill Harry saw what was coming and fled to his office around the corner in Oxford Street. It was a wise move. He heard they planned to tie him up with rope and suspend him upside down out of the window above the street.

Zeppelin's terrified publicist locked the door and listened with fear and dread as doors were broken down and furniture strewn down the stairs. Thwarted in their pursuit of Bill Harry, Bonham and Webb set upon the managing director of Chrysalis Records and bound him from the neck down in Sellotape, until he was mummified and then dumped him wriggling and helpless on the pavement in London's main shopping thoroughfare.

The mummy reminded them of the Middle East, and they decided to rush down to Covent Garden and hire a set of Arab outfits from a theatrical costumiers. Suitably attired, they adjourned to the Prince Of Wales pub where they outraged lady patrons by raising their robes to reveal naked loins.

Inspiration struck Bonham and he booked his party of fake Arab princes into the Maharajah suite of the Mayfair Hotel. Cabbies and hotel porters saluted the visiting potentates, imagining some oil riches might flow their way.

The suite was decorated with a stuffed tiger, rich tapestries and priceless furniture. On their way up to this splendid setting, the 'Arabs', so far forgot themselves once more to raise their robes in front of some visiting American blue rinse women, who promptly set about them with umbrellas.

Inside the suite John ordered fifty steaks for his chums and within minutes of their arrival, the steaks were flying around the room. Much damage was caused to the tiger and a colour telly. The party were ejected and subsequently John Bonham was blacklisted and barred from all the major hotels in London. The wandering Arabs eventually ended up in their by now bedraggled robes, at the Speakeasy, where the hardened customers totally ignored them.

But Bonzo had not forgotten how Bill Harry had managed to elude him. Sometime later there occurred an incident which finally caused Bill to hand in his notice. 'I just blew my cool and couldn't stand it anymore. I could take hijinks and the funny things. But I got depressed at the jokes on me all the time. I was doing publicity for Suzie Quatro as well, and was with her in the Coach & Horses one lunch time. Suddenly a call came through. John Bonham was coming to town and wanted to do an interview – NOW.'

In vain Bill did explain it was a time when most newspaper offices were empty, but eventually he managed to get hold of Roy Carr who cheerfully agreed to rush round for an exclusive chat with Zeppelin's drummer. The pair were put safely together in a corner of the pub while Bill carried on chatting with Suzie Quatro. Maybe this division of loyalties upset Bonzo.

'I went back to Suzie and we were just leaving. I had all my loose change and wallet in my back pocket. I just walked past the table where Roy Carr and John Bonham were sitting. I said "Everything okay? I'm leaving now. See you later." John reached out and ripped the back pocket off my trousers. All my money went spinning round the pub while Suzie was watching from the door.'

It was the final straw to break the publicist's back.

'I said "Look, you keep doing things like this, and I don't need this. I don't want to have anything more to do with you from this moment on. If you're coming down the street, go to the other side, I don't want to see you.'

Bill got a call from Peter Grant who said: 'You go and buy the most expensive pair of trousers you can find and put it on the bill.' Said Bill: 'Thanks for the offer Peter but I don't want to do the group anymore.' He could no longer take the pressure and he was replaced by Irish deejay, journalist and publicist, B. P. Fallon. Said Bill with some delight: 'I heard he bought this fantastic green velvet suit which was very expensive. Zeppelin got hold of him and threw him in the swimming pool, in his suit. He probably sent them the bill.'

Reflected Bill on his bust up with Zeppelin: 'I couldn't take it any-more. It had annoyed me, in front of a pub full of people, to have somebody rip my trousers and to have to get down on the floor and pick up money. But John was a great guy really. He probably didn't even mean to rip the pocket off. Bonzo used to go out drinking with Keith Moon and it would be all the lads together having a laugh. But I was a family man by then, with a kid coming and I wanted to settle down.

'A period of my life was coming to an end. I had to stop boozing and gigging. I'd spent a decade going out every night of the week. So it wasn't just the incident with John. I was getting too old to be carousing around all the time. But it was amazing the booze we used to drink . . . fifty lagers in one session . . . I could never imagine doing it now.'

There was one little incident when Bill Harry had the chance to chuckle at Zeppelin's expense. 'I remember a gig in Holland. The band were on a massive stage and the hall was packed with thousands of kids. The sound was crystal clear. You could hear everything. Suddenly – in the middle of a number – Robert Plant farted. You could hear it clearly. Unbelievable to hear a rock star fart on stage. Everyone stood there stunned then broke up laughing. And it was totally unrehearsed.'

Back in America in the early part of 1975 the band got down to the serious business of making music, not mayhem. But when MM writer Chris Charlesworth went to see the band play at the Chicago Stadium he discovered that Jimmy Page was taking pain killer tablets for the injured finger, still causing distress after his accident with a train door.

Said Jimmy: 'I can't play any blues at all, and can't bend notes either. It's the most important finger for any guitarist, so I'm having to modify my playing to suit the situation. A shame but it can't be helped. We had to cut *Dazed And Confused* from the set and substitute *How Many More Times* which we haven't played for four years. I can't play the violin bow as well as I'd like. We almost cancelled the tour but we couldn't as we'd sold all the tickets and a postponement would have meant chaos. It couldn't have happened at a worse time either.'

A roadie told Chris: 'It takes them a few concerts to get into stride, but by the time this band gets to Madison Square Garden it'll be one of the best rock acts ever to set foot there.'

The band's three hour show included five new songs from *Physical Graffiti*. The album's release had been delayed due to artwork problems. It was due out in Britain February 25, their sixth album and the first on Swan Song. It went gold and platinum on the day of its release and went straight to Number One in the Billboard chart. In America alone it brought in twelve million dollars within a year. Not only was *Physical Graffiti* a huge hit, it also revitalised the back catalogue of Zeppelin albums all of which reappeared at various positions on the US charts.

101

This was truly rock's finest hour. Bands like Zeppelin, Wings, The Stones, Yes and Genesis seemed to rule the world. Within a year there would be the punk rock backlash, and then a catastrophic business slump in the western world. Things would never be quite the same again. Meanwhile, before the storm clouds closed in, rock enjoyed its Indian summer.

Physical Graffiti was a double album and consisted of new material with tracks from previous album sessions. The over riding impression was of the band's most consistent and impressive work since *Led Zeppelin III*.

Tracks included *Custard Pie, The Rover, In My Time Of Dying, Houses Of The Holy, Trampled Underfoot, Kashmir, In The Light, Bron-Y-Aur, Down By The Seaside, Ten Years Gone, Night Plight, The Wanton Song, Boogie With Stu, Black Country Woman* and *Sick Again*. Of the older material *Bron-y-Aur* was from *Led Zeppelin III* sessions, while *Black Country Woman* and *The Rover* were planned for inclusion on the *Houses Of The Holy* LP.

Said Jimmy: 'As usual we had more material than the forty odd minutes for one album. We had enough for one and a half LPs, so we put out a double and used some of the material we had done previously but never released.'

There were a million advance orders and most critics agreed it was a powerful album, possibly the best in their career. Robert talked to Chris Charlesworth about the album when the band were in New York. 'I suppose it was about a year ago when we started it. It's always a case of getting together and feeling out the moods of each of us when we meet with instruments for the first time in six months . . . we began as always playing around and fooling about for two days, playing anything we want, like standards of our own material or anything that comes to us. Slowly we develop a feel that takes us into the new material.

'Some of the new stuff came directly from this approach like *Trampled Underfoot* which was just blowing out, and some comes from Jonesey or Pagey or myself – seldom myself – bringing along some structure which needs working on. Then the four of us inflict our own venom on it to develop ideas.'

Robert admitted that 1974 was a year of little Zeppelin activity mainly because they wanted to spend time at home. 'I wanted to take stock of everything instead of going on the road until I don't know where I am and end up like a poached egg, three days old. We all needed that time off, but cursed each other for having it and agreed at the same time we had been physically idle.'

Robert explained that the group actually hated rehearsing but had to limber up somehow. 'The first hour is usually great, but then we think how much better it would be if there was an audience there. A lot of the

102

construction that we do on stage is fired by the atmosphere of the moment. Obviously we had to rehearse the stuff from the new album to get it into some viable shape. We played all the new songs at the rehearsal, but some of them take such a direction that it would be difficult to employ them live after being off the road for eighteen months.

'We do *Sick Again* which is about ourselves and what we see in Los Angeles. The lyrics say: "From the window of a rented limousine, I saw your pretty blue eyes. One day soon you're gonna reach sixteen, painted lady in the city of lies." It's sour really. That's exactly what LA stands for. Joni Mitchell summed it up best when whe called it City Of The Fallen Angels.'

Robert talked a little about their reputation as hell raisers. 'Like the music, the legend grows too. There are times when people need outlets. We don't rehearse them and let's face it everybody's the same. Over the last few years we've spent some of our time at the Edgewater Inn in Seattle where Bonzo fishes for sharks in the sea from his bedroom window. Hence the mudshark thing on the Zappa album. No, we're not calming down yet. Calming down doesn't exist until you're dead. You just do whatever you want to do, provided there's no nastiness involved, then the karma isn't so good...'

In direct contrast to their heavy image, was the success of the ballad *Stairway To Heaven* still being played non-stop on US radio and said Robert: 'It's quite a moving thing. I can remember doing it at the Garden when I sang well away from the mike and I could hear 20,000 people singing it. I mean ... 20,000 people singing *High Heel Sneakers* is one thing but 20,000 singing *Stairway To Heaven* is another. People leave satisfied after that and I don't think they leave because of the violent aspects of the music, which I don't think exist anyway.'

Robert Plant later summed up the reaction to the album and the US tour: 'Aside from the fact it's been our most successful tour on every level I just found myself having a great time all the way through. The music gelled amazingly well. Everyone loved *Physical Graffiti*. That meant a lot. It's like we're on an incredible winning streak. It's not just that we think we're the best group in the world. It's just that we think we're so much better than whoever is Number Two.'

In April tickets for the Earls Court shows due in May went on sale. Some 51,000 sold within two hours. Another two nights were added to the three planned and another 34,000 tickets sold over a weekend.

The concerts were the first in Britain since January 1973 and there was massive press coverage with supplements and special issues in the national as well as the music press. I went to see their show on Saturday with mixed feelings. There were no tickets made available for the Melody Maker by promoter Mel Bush, despite the fact that Melody

103

Maker put the band on the cover, devoted a four page special feature to them and had given the album a rave review. It seemed memories of my review of *Houses Of The Holy* had not yet faded. Eventually I gained access to the hall, twenty minutes after the concert started, and sat on the grimy steps of a gangway. Fortunately the brilliance of their music and excitement of the show made up for the discomfort, hassles and the occasional grumbles directed at me from Robert. I still couldn't believe they had taken such umbrage at my review, especially as years later I read American reviews of *Houses Of The Holy* which were far more scathing than mine. C'est la vie.

The programme, a distinctive red and yellow affair had a drawing of a Victorian steam engine called *Physical Rocket* on the cover. The inside notes were equally quaint. The writer in his introduction proclaimed: 'Led Zeppelin's music, stylistically, is a tour de force, borrowing from Bo Diddley, The Stones, Cream, Burt Bacharach and Kool and the Gang; a fusion of jazz, rock, blues and flamenco.'

Kool and the Gang? Flamenco? The mind boggled.

Originally Mel Bush had talked to Zeppelin about the possibility of doing a national tour, but they made it clear they wanted to put on the show they had been doing in America. Earls Court was the only venue big enough. The band flew over their equipment on a private jet. With the laser lighting and huge PA system it was reckoned the show cost around £30,000 a night to put on. The hire of the hall cost £5,000. The staging was by Showco of Dallas, Texas and they provided a fifteen man stage crew. As well as installing the equipment they had to meet the hall and local council regulations about fire and safety, all of which had to be checked by the promoter.

Said Ian Wright, the stage director: 'People automatically believe Led Zeppelin are going to earn a fortune from these shows. Well they're not. Not when you compare the sheer expense of staging such an event in ratio to the low ticket prices. Zeppelin can consider themselves lucky if they break even. The overheads are incredibly high.'

Whatever the pros and cons of putting on the shows, Zeppelin played with a fire that surprised even the band, which had after all been on the road since January. In my review I wrote: 'Laser beams, green pencils of light cut through the smoke surrounding Jimmy Page, as the master guitarist of rock flailed a violin bow against the strings, filling the cavern of Earls Court with an eerie howl of Gothic horror. It was one of the most vivid moments etched on the memory of a remarkable tour de force when Led Zeppelin came among us like avenging angels at the weekend.'

Others described how the show and its powerful images were 'burned onto their brain' and I called it a 'three hour cauldron of events'. If there is any truth at all in the power of magic, then it is not an exaggeration to say that Zeppelin seemed to possess mysterious power over its audience during those nights at Earls Court.

I wrote: 'Robert Plant maintains an essentially human chatty approach to audiences, almost like a guide taking us through the story of the band, a jester at the wheel of some fearsome juggernaut, offering sly asides and poetic ruminations between moments of terrible power.'

I reported that one of the most exciting moments of the whole show was their sensational performance of *Trampled Underfoot*. 'The band seemed much more at home and gained most satisfaction from the new material while their greatest moments with older songs came with the ballads and acoustic melodies like *Stairway To Heaven* and *Tangerine*. John Paul Jones surprised everybody with his piano solo on *No Quarter* which presented the normally reticent bass player in a whole new light.' It was noted that John Paul Jones had a lot to do with the increased range of sounds Zeppelin now had at their command. There were more keyboards in evidence and an orchestral flavour did justice to the broad sweep of the band's new arrangements.

A huge screen above the stage displayed 'live' instant pictures of the band in colour and the close ups, particularly those of Robert's anatomy, were better than those afforded by front row seats. The screen cost £4,000, was custom built for the band, and was the largest in the world. Nifty camera work showed us Jimmy's fluent finger work and the cavalcade of expressions flowing across Plant's face. Bare chested, laughing, Robert seemed to be enjoying himself hugely. Even when there were grumbles from the back of the hall when the group sat down for the acoustic set, Robert refused to be upset. 'Oh I knew this would go down well,' he said wryly. 'This is just like Grateful Dead's set.' There were more mutterings. 'Shut up a bit' and then swiftly, 'give us a kiss'.

Later Robert began a deadpan rap about how Robert Johnson the famed bluesman was responsible for the next item on the agenda. John Bonham expressed his impatience and broke the spell with a sudden cry of 'Bollocks!' Robert gave way with a burst of laughter and the band tore into *Trampled Underfoot*.

This was an amazing performance, a real soul stomp and one of those riffs that could go on all night. But there was a lot more to come, including an astounding *Moby Dick* drum solo from Bonzo about which I waxed eloquent in the Melody Maker for about eight paragraphs.

After this barrage of drumming, Robert stepped up and presented Bonzo with the traditional banana. I thought a pint of beer would have been more appropriate. 'This is the first thing we ever played together,' said Robert leading into *Dazed And Confused*. There came a flash and a puff of smoke as Jimmy unleashed those tearing, electrifying opening remarks on guitar, and snatched up his violin bow. I wrote: 'The drama was heightened by the converging beams of laser light that threatened

105

to vaporise Mr Page before our eyes.'

Next came the fast, free improvised guitar solo with bass and drums scampering in hot pursuit, with a pause of breath to bring in *Stairway To Heaven*. A mirror ball above the stage started to revolve, bathing the auditorium in light as the group backed off stage and Robert said 'Goodnight everybody . . . it's been great.'

The realisation that the show was over brought a roar and pounding of feet that lasted six minutes. Maybe ten. When the house lights went up there was a great booing. Hastily the lights dimmed and the stage lit up with a giant 'Led Zeppelin' sign, while the band dashed back into view. 'Sorry about the delay, but we had to have a cup of tea,' explained Robert shamelessly.

There was only one number that could follow . . . *Whole Lotta Love*. But there was one more secret weapon to be brought into play: 'Like some sorcerer's apprentice Jimmy flung aside his guitar to make magic passes with his hands before a giant wand rising perpendicular from the stage. Weird noises emerged in response to his shimmering palms and the device seemed to work on a similar principle to my TV aerial that blacks out the screen if the cat sits on it. And lo the show was over, with only the slow shuffle of myriad feet across the boards and gangways to mark the presence of an audience which only seconds before had been bellowing like men possessed. I summed up the show thus: 'It was a splendid return proof that Zeppelin have their strength and imagination intact, and a great zest for fresh challenges. It's looking good for the next six years of Zeppelin history making.' And there of course, I was very wrong.

Zeppelin would continue to make history and news but not quite in the way I envisaged.

During the Earls Court shows Robert had dedicated *In Time Of Dying* to that most taxing of politicians, Chancellor Denis Healey who was busy taking a large percentage of rock star earnings. The band chose to become tax exiles and live abroad for a while. After the London dates Robert's first priority however was a family holiday in Morocco. Later he met Jimmy and the pair went for a drive in a Range Rover through the Sahara desert. They carried their trip on across to Europe, through Spain and France to Montreux where they met the group and Peter Grant to plan another American tour. The idea was to play thirty-three dates in the States starting on August 23, with a trip to South America added on. After attending the Montreux jazz festival, Page and Plant and respective families headed for the Greek island of Rhodes.

On August 3 Jimmy left to go to Italy and planned to meet the whole band again in Paris a few days later to begin rehearsing for the tour. But the following day, Robert was involved in a serious accident. His hired car hit a tree. Robert's wife Maureen had a fractured pelvis and skull, and Robert had multiple fractures of ankle and elbow. Their two children Karac and Carmen travelling in the back seat escaped with only minor injuries. They were taken to hospital on the back of a truck and later air lifted home for treatment. Robert was told that he couldn't walk again for at least six months, and Maureen was concussed for thirty-six hours.

The world tour which would have taken up their time as British tax exiles had to be cancelled and Robert only just escaped from England to Jersey before his time at home expired. He would have been due for a full year's tax. After a spell in Jersey, he moved to California and stayed in a beach house in Malibu. After a while he began to hobble around on crutches and eventually Jimmy Page came over to Malibu to start writing songs. It was the best kind of therapy. Said Robert: 'We have all this time now, why don't we use it and make an album?'

In October John Paul Jones (who had recently broken his hand) and John Bonham joined Page and Plant and began rehearsing in Los Angeles.

The band recorded the album in Musicland Studios, Munich and it was completed with a surprising burst of speed. There were no distractions, and with Robert's leg in plaster, he certainly wasn't going anywhere else. In fact there was nearly another accident when Robert became over-excited during a number and ran towards the recording booth. He fell over despite his crutch and landed on his bad foot. He folded up in agony while Jimmy came to his rescue and rushed him off to hospital. There were fears the healing process had been set back and that Robert might never walk again. But by December he was able to walk about unaided. He even managed a brief and unexpected appearance in a night club with John Bonham. It was in Behan's Night Club in Jersey, backing a pianist Norman Hale, who had once been a member of the Tornadoes, famed for their hit with *Telstar*. Robert sat on a stool and sang, while Zeppelin played for forty-five minutes to 350 people.

In Paris on New Year's Eve Robert took his first unaided steps and joked 'One small step for man, one giant leap for six nights at Madison Square Garden.' He revealed that the new album would be called *Presence* and said 'The album is full of energy because of that sort of primal fight within me, to get back, to get better. There is a lot of determination on the album, and fist banging on the table.'

The album came out, late as usual, on April 6, 1976 and went straight to Number One in the British chart, while in America it reached Number One a week after release. Tracks on *Presence* included *Achilles Last Stand, For Your Life, Royal Orleans, Nobody's Fault But Mine, Candy Store Rock, Hots On For Nowhere* and *Tea For One*. The album cover featured a strange 'Obelisk', a twisted piece of sculpture featured in a series of unrelated pictures culled from Fifties American life. It was one of

Hipgnosis' more enigmatic designs.

During the summer the band surfaced in the news for various activities, from jamming with Bad Company on their American dates to 'insulting' actor Telly Savalas on a flight across the Atlantic. There were more ructions when filmmaker Kenneth Anger complained that Jimmy Page hadn't finished the music for his film *Lucifer Rising*. It was alleged he had only composed twenty-eight minutes of music in three years of work on the project. Said Anger: 'The way he has been behaving is totally contradictory to the teachings of Aleister Crowley and the ethos of the film.' Jimmy said the whole thing was absurd. He assumed that Anger hadn't yet finished the film: 'Anger's time was all that was needed to finish that film. Nothing else!'

Much to the surprise of all Zeppelin fans, another new album was released, just a few months after *Presence*. This was unheard of activity. It was in fact a 'live' double album of the soundtrack from *The Song Remains The Same* which appeared on October 18. On October 20 the world premiere of the movie took place at New York's Cinema One, which raised twenty-five thousand dollars for a children's charity. The British premiere was held in two cinemas in London's West End on November 4. I went to the premiere and thoroughly enjoyed the film, although some of the 'fantasy' sequences used to break up the action were a shade precious. John Bonham came off the best as a drag racing driver, while Jimmy's clamber up the mountainsides didn't really work. Some rock critics at last had the excuse to launch into fierce attacks on the band, with all the bile built up over the years of success when there was little basis for criticism. Dave Marsh, of Rolling Stone, grumbled that the film was a 'tribute to their rapaciousness and inconsideration. While Led Zeppelin's music remains worthy of respect (even if their best songs are behind them) their sense of themselves merits only contempt.' It was interesting to note that Marsh could predict the contents of their next album before it was conceived, written or recorded.

Jimmy Page answered criticism of the film, saying: 'It's not a great film, just a reasonably honest statement of where we were at a particular time. That's all it can be really.'

Peter Grant cheerfully described it as 'the most expensive home movie ever made.'

Even while Zeppelin were celebrating on film the triumphs of a Madison Square appearance of a few years before in 1973, there were strange rumblings of discontent within the rock world. The supremacy of groups epitomised by Zeppelin – flash, rich and powerful – was being undermined by the appearance of the new wave, the underground, punks and the Sex Pistols. It was the old Andrew Oldham/ Rolling Stones outrage hype dredged up for consumption by victims of the recession, but there were many business interests happy to see the establishment overturned, abused and discomforted. Curiously enough, Zeppelin and most of the groups never actually saw themselves as targets for such cries as 'boring old farts' and 'dinosaur group' mainly dreamed up by bored news editors anxious to finish off the usual filler items before diving off to the pub.

During January 1977 the band rehearsed for a forthcoming tour in a converted cinema in London's Fulham Road. In the evening Robert and Jimmy went to see such new stars as The Damned at The Roxy in Covent Garden and announced their approval. They denied there was any difference between the inherent feeling in Zeppelin or The Damned's music. They'd just been doing it a bit longer. But while there was little real animosity between the groups, the music press, taking their cue from fanzines, desperately sought 'street credibility'. Thus they launched into ever more vitriolic attacks on all kinds of music, even punk itself, until in the end there was nothing left much left to destroy except each other and their own newspapers. Stripped of goodwill, credibility and circulation, they were largely superceded by simplistic colour pop weeklies, and children's TV programmes which provided the necessary service of news and information. The great edifice of rock journalism collapsed.

Led Zeppelin and their fellow British groups found themselves strangers in a strange land.

EIGHT

███████

THE
SONG
IS
ENDED

███████

The Song Remains The Same was the last brash expression of confidence by Led Zeppelin before they were knocked sideways by a succession of blows. Quite apart from their public following, the band were still fashionable and their position as top dogs of the rock industry unassailable. During the New York premiere of their full length film, sections of the audience broke into spontaneous applause, like Russians greeting news of higher tractor production. Whenever one of the group tried to slink out of the theatre for a moment, he was followed by packs of fans. Outside in the street, traffic came to a standstill as waiting crowds surged around the building.

After the screening, at a cinema on Third Avenue, a party was held at the Pierre Hotel Cafe, where the Seventies elite paid homage to the band, including Mick Jagger, Simon Kirke, Carly Simon, Rick Derringer, Mick Ronson and Roberta Flack.

The film was a product of its time, a period when people were in awe of the power of rock music, the wealth it generated, and the vast following it could command. 'Rock music is now bigger than the movie industry' was the excited cry to be heard from coast to coast. It seemed logical that rock stars should also be able to exercise their stage magic on the big screen. In fact, the band were ahead of their time. Rock would eventually forge a more successful alliance – with video and on a smaller screen. Zeppelin's 'fantasy sequences' in *The Song Remains The Same*

110

became extended into an art form in the more managable and cost effective three minute promo 'videos' of the Eighties, many of them actually shot on film to obtain better quality.

The bulk of Zeppelin's epic was devoted to the band's concert at Madison Square Garden three years earlier, and serves as a unique record of the band in action. Most fascinating however was the material shot backstage showing the harder face of Zeppelin.

One scene showed Peter Grant involved in a heated argument with a concessionaire at The Garden, about the sale of 'pirate' photographs of the group. This touch of *cinema verité* was linked with the fantasy scenes. The first showed Peter as a Mafia-style Godfather hellbent on wiping out a rival gang, with henchman Richard Cole, all dressed Chicago style. After the subsequent bloodbath, and the credits, Peter was seen in more realistic mode, on the phone arranging details for a tour. The band were shown relaxing in various home environments.

Robert and his wife Maureen were seen sporting in the country; John Paul read bedtime stories to his kids; John Bonham drove a tractor and Jimmy Page fished a Scottish stream.

Telegrams fetched the band from their hideaway and they dashed to America by plane and limo, to appear on stage at Madison Square in front of cheering hordes.

The band's fantasies were played out during each member's solo spot in the concert. Thus, John Paul was shown during *No Quarter*, Robert in *The Song Remains The Same*, Jimmy in *Dazed And Confused* and John Bonham during *Moby Dick*.

Robert chose to appear as a Viking explorer, arriving on a beach at night, accepting a sword from a woman on a horse in the lake. His mission was to rescue a maid in distress from a nearby castle. John Paul was also involved in horse play, as a night rider in a grotesque mask, terrifying the local yokels, in between bouts of Bach on the church organ.

Jimmy climbed through a wood and up a steep hill where a hermit awaited, who proved to be an aged, wizened version of himself, brandishing swords. Bonham's sequence was more down to earth. No swords or fair maids, but a prize cow and a drag racing car, his drum solo matching the roar of the car accelerating down the course. All agreed his was the most successful.

Apart from its general entertainment value, the film tried to hint at the uneasy clash of idealism and business interests that made Zeppelin so formidable and difficult to understand. For example a TV news clip showed the press conference after the theft of 200,000 dollars from the New York hotel in 1973. Together with the scenes of Peter arguing, it seemed to confirm to outsiders that Zeppelin were too big for their boots.

111

In October 1976 while Zeppelin were still making the front pages of the British music press and winning polls, inside there were reviews of a new breed of bands, like The Clash, and news that the Sex Pistols had signed a record contract and were 'on their way' according to the Melody Maker's astute Caroline Coon.

An early TV documentary on punk included a shot of a wild-eyed punk shouting abuse about Led Zeppelin trampling over everyone and getting rich in the process, contrary to the ideals of the new movement. Keen observers noted the 'punk' demanding retribution on the head of Peter Grant, was a one-time Sixties hippie and record producer. It seemed there were quite a few using punk rock to settle old scores.

In November 1976 I met Jimmy Page at Swan Song's office in the New King's Road. He greeted me with a warm handshake and twinkling eyes, and exuded good cheer. Shortly after I mentioned this in a subsequent article I received a letter from Kenneth Anger accusing me of 'hype' and suggesting that a 'cold clammy handshake' was more likely.

Jimmy talked about the film and how he enjoyed watching it at the New York premiere with an enthusiastic audience. I asked if he thought it had achieved all their aims when they first conceived the film.

'Yeah pretty much. Obviously there were things that weren't quite the way we wanted them. It's a massive compromise making films. You can just go on spending a fortune. The fantasy sequences were introduced because we had gaps in the film of the performance and we coudn't really cut the soundtrack because so much of our stuff is improvised.' Jimmy explained that the sequences had grown during filming, in the same way that their album tracks took place in the studio.

'It was like when we each chose a symbol for the fourth album. We each went away and came up with an idea. It gave insight into each personality, whether it was tongue-in-cheek or deadly serious.'

Jimmy's mountaineering was presumably in the latter category. 'Yeah, it was a bit hairy actually. It wasn't done in one take – that was the trouble.

'It was a very steep climb at this place in Scotland, and it didn't occur to me that I'd have to go and do it again! The crew said "Back down there" . . . and believe me, it was very steep, and I've got a great fear of heights. I wanted to get a full moon in the shot and it came up in December. I thought it would be great in snow so there would be a luminescent quality. Curiously enough the night we arrived was a full moon and blow me if there wasn't snow on the mountain. But they didn't get the cameras up in time and the snow had melted by the next night. It wouldn't have worked anyway.'

How important was making the movie to Zeppelin's career?

'An incredible challenge because we are not a bunch of chaps that compromise easily. Having got over the hurdle of making it, it's exhilar-

112

ating to feel the response. New York was incredible. It's a great relief that it's out.'

Jimmy was most excited at the prospect of touring again in 1977. 'We have already started rehearsals. The world tour we were going to embark on was going to include places like Cairo but that didn't come together. We'd still like to do that one day because you've gotta have change, you can't stand still. We're starting the tour in February in the States but I don't know when we'll be back in England. Obviously next year sometime, but I don't know exactly when. The main thing is we're bursting to get back on the road, as you may well imagine. That *Presence* album really did us so much good. When you've been together that long and embark on an LP, whatever we've got ready, we say "Forget about that, we'll go straight in". And the spontaneity of rehearsals in the studio brings out the best in us. To come up with all that stuff after a frustrating and emotional period, and to find it was all there was marvellous. You see we were only a week or so away from the first date of a tour when Robert's accident happened. Suddenly we were let down, not knowing at all what was coming in the future. There was a great amount of uncertainty. Now the group is very tight. There is a great feeling in the band y'know. We'll be going on for years. The good feelings are still there. You never know what is going to come around the corner next and that's the whole magic of it.'

While fans had cheered the movie at its premiere and MM's Chris Charlesworth had called it 'honest, heavy and hot' not all reviewers were convinced. American film critics while impressed by the standard of photography, sound and lighting, were unmoved by the band's contribution. Said one reviewer: '*The Song Remains The Same* is overall, not only a bad rock 'n' roll film but a poor representation of Led Zeppelin's musical abilities'. Peter Oppel in the Dallas Morning News complained: 'The most glaring fault with the movie is that although it purports to be a live concert it isn't. The music heard on the soundtrack ninty-nine percent of it anyway – was not recorded at Madison Square Garden but overdubbed and perfected in the studio. As a result the entire affair is sterile. Led Zeppelin is an overpowering concert act. Because of the overdubbing they are anything but overpowering in this movie. You can see the energy put forth on stage, but it doesn't translate to the soundtrack. The movie is full of meaningless scenes. The fantasy sequences may be beautifully photographed but what do we learn about Led Zeppelin from them? Absolutely nothing . . . The makers of this film have accomplished the impossible – they have made Led Zeppelin boring.'

Jimmy admitted to me that the band had much better 'live' stuff than was apparent on the soundtrack and subsequent *Song Remains The Same* album. 'Obviously we were committed to putting this album out

113

although it wasn't necessarily the best live stuff we have. I've been working on a lot at home. I've got a couple of long pieces that would make good albums. We've got six live concerts on tape which were good nights. We've got some ancient stuff, live at the Royal Albert Hall in 1969, and it's very interesting to listen to now. You can compare different versions of tunes as they span a couple of years. A chronological compilation is the thing I've always been keen on, but the soundtrack came instead, so that can be shelved for a while.'

I asked Jimmy if he felt, like the movie critics, that the film could have shown more about the running of the band, and more glimpses of their manager at work behind the scenes? 'Well we were rather dubious about putting something like that down. The scene featuring Peter was pretty honest I thought. Possibly we could have had more of that, but what we wanted most was for the pace to build. If you have a helluva lot of dialogue, then you stop the music altogether. We were trying to keep the music going as much as possible.

'We didn't want interviews with each member of the group. We were going to leave out the New York hotel robbery but it was a documentary. It was all true. It happened.'

I suggested that the film had started out as a documentary and then shied away from it. 'Well it was a montage, wasn't it? That was the challenge to keep it from just being a concert, and I think it's a fair old balance. It could be interesting to do a full documentary on that side of the group y'know, what goes down. But it's a taste. Get your imagination working!'

The following April, after Robert had recovered from a bout of tonsilitis, they began their eleventh trip to America. Although it began with great expectations and good humour, it would be marred by tragedy and brought to a sudden, dramatic end.

The tour was their biggest yet, with fifty-one concerts in thirty cities scheduled and over a million fans ready to cheer them on their way. It began in Dallas in April 1, 1977, and fanned around the country, with the band playing over three hours a night and using the video projection screen at the larger venues. Tickets were selling at the rate of 72,000 a day, and Zep broke all records on April 30 when they performed at the Pontiac Silverdome in front of 76,229 fans who paid eight hundred thousand dollars. It was the largest audience ever for a single rock band.

But already there were rumblings. The American Circus magazine early in the year referred to Led Zeppelin's previous run of bad luck, including Robert's car crash, as a 'karmic collision course', hinting that there was something odd about the accidents that seemed to pursue the band members. It was noted that Jimmy Page seemed much healthier than he had been on previous tours and was taking a daily mixture of banana daiquiri and protein. Robert told reporters: 'We've got a new

Jimmy Page. He's the leader again. And if he doesn't stay healthy – I'll kill him!'

However, during one of four nights at the Chicago Stadium, Jimmy had to sit down while playing *Ten Years Gone* and after an hour of the concert, the band called a halt, and sent for medical advice. Then a fleet of limos rushed the entourage back to the Ambassador East Hotel, with a police escort. Jimmy said he had to stop playing due to 'unbearable agony' caused by food poisoning.

Many could see that Jimmy was painfully thin, unable to eat solid food, and was beginning to age, with grey flecking his black tousled hair. He told reporters: 'It's the first time we've ever stopped a gig like that. We always have a go, because we're not a rip-off band. But the pain was unbearable. If I hadn't sat down I would have fallen over.' Jimmy emphasised that the band was enjoying its tour despite the bouts of illness and delays. It's good out on the tiles, away from home. It's a stag party that never ends. And it's been great to get back on the road after all the trials and tribulations that have been a hazard for over a year. It's great to see the smiles. This is no last tour. We're here and we'll always come back. It would be a criminal act to break up this band.'

'The worst thing for us would be if we were considered a nostalgia band.' Jimmy told Lisa Robinson. 'But I don't think we are. One stays contemporary by changing. Going out on a limb all the time is very rewarding. I don't care about being 'fashionable' All that posing is just amusing. As for our popularity I think it's very flattering to be able to sell out all these concerts. We've gone through so many changes, and people have been able to relate to them and still come and see us. We hadn't played for two years and I always get stage fright anyway. But the worst thing was we were rehearsing to come over to the States when Robert got tonsilitis. All the equipment had been sent on ahead for the tour. I didn't touch an instrument for about a month, so naturally for the first few dates I was quite nervous.'

Not all critics were pleased with Zeppelin's showing on the tour. They complained that it was too long, the solos went on at too great a length, and some felt that Robert's singing on the acoustic numbers 'lacked soul'. Others criticised Jimmy's guitar work.

The band felt otherwise. Said Jimmy: 'There were some tremendous moments . . . It was very intense . . . we were tight, yet loose, loosely tight.'

Certainly they seemed in the mood for their legendary brand of horseplay. Robert Plant's suite at the Ambassador East Hotel in Chicago was described by one eyewitness as 'a room with wall to wall hamburger patties, Cola drenched bedsheets, french fried plastered walls, mustard smeared mirrors, a sixteen piece telephone and gutted cusions where the furniture used to be.' Robert confessed they had been moved

115

to commit such acts of vandalism and mindless violence – at their own expense – out of boredom and for pleasure. 'You know on some nights after a gig, it's just like the 1973 tour. We've already equalled that in our short stay. It goes as far as it does because it's a laugh. It's not any release. All that about road fever is just bullshit. We only do what we do because it's fun. The lifestyle of rock 'n' roll is to live well and take a good woman.' It also apparently included John Bonham going from bedroom to bedroom armed with a broken piece of furniture to finish off each room in turn.

Throughout the tour there were riots and arrests as fans without tickets tried to gatecrash shows. Some of the worst trouble started at Tampa Stadium on June 3 when the concert had to be cancelled after only twenty minutes because of rain. It was pouring onto the stage and the band feared electrocution.

The show started well but soon police with riot gear arrived and began bashing heads and kicking fans. Over a hundred fans and seventeen police were injured after the group quit the stage during the rainstorm. The Mayor announced that Zeppelin would be banned forever from appearing in Tampa for the 'health and protection of police and citizens'.

Reporter Jack Lyons wrote in Rock Scene: 'It all started innocently enough; fans drove from as far as Illinois, New York and Georgia, waving to each other with one thought in their minds – Led Zeppelin. The much publicised concert began as the rock group hit the stage at 8.20pm. "This is our first trip to Tampa in four years," said bare chested Robert Plant, his huge penis bulging in his pants. "It's good to be back."

'The band had barely played *The Song Remains The Same* before lightning ripped through the sky and rain poured in a drenching torrent. "We have to stop or our equipment will blow up," yelled Robert.'

Midway through the tour the band had fitted in a seventeen day break. Jimmy sloped off to Cairo to see the pyramids, while the rest of the band and their manager went to a showbiz lunch in London where they were given an Ivor Novello Award for their contribution to British music.

Back in the States they played six nights at Madison Square Garden in New York from June 7-14 followed by six nights, from June 21-27 at the Los Angeles Forum. With wild audience reaction and fans everywhere begging for tickets it seemed Zeppelin were on top of the world.

Then at the Oakland Coliseum on July 23 came a violent scene which shocked Zeppelin fans. The horseplay turned to rough stuff and a nasty fracas when Peter Grant, John Bonham and a bodyguard, John Bindon, attacked one of promoter Bill Graham's security men.

The security man had apparently refused to give Peter's son a name

116

plate from a dressing room door on a caravan, which he wanted as a souvenir. Richard Cole was also involved in an alleged assault on another of Graham's employees. All three were arrested, charged with assault and then freed on bail. The criminal charges were followed up by a threatened civil action to sue them for two million dollars. The security man was hospitalised.

The band flew on to New Orleans where they were due to play at the Superdome. Then on July 26 came even worse news. Robert's son Karac, aged five, had fallen ill at home in England with a mysterious stomach infection. The following day he got worse, and was taken by ambulance to hospital, but was dead on arrival. Robert immediately flew back to England and the rest of the tour dates were cancelled. Robert was met at Birmingham Airport by his father who told reporters: 'All this success and fame. What is it worth? It doesn't seem much when you compare it to the love of a family.'

Many thought this signalled the end of the band although at first it was believed the group would try to finish off the tour with concerts in Buffalo, Philadelphia, Chicago and Pittsburg. It was not to be. More details of the fracas began to emerge. It was reported that there were three separate instances of Grant, Bonham or their aides allegedly beating up a production manager, stagehand and security guard during the first of two shows at the Oakland Stadium in California. Bill Graham tried to stop the fighting without success. He later stated that representatives of the group informed him the group would not show up for the second show unless Graham signed an indemnification, guaranteeing he would pay any judgements found against the defendents in lawsuits over the incidents.

Graham signed and the show went on, eighty minutes late. He was worried about the possibility of a riot if the show was cancelled at such a late stage. He was also told by his own attorney that the indemnification wouldn't hold up in court.

In the midst of such turmoil it was inevitable that there would be much speculation and rumour. I was at a London rock concert when a man who claimed to be an ex-Zeppelin roadie approached me and said quite categorically that the group had actually killed a security man during the Oakland assault. I declined to believe him. It was hardly the sort of thing even a powerful rock band could cover up. There would be the matter of eyewitnesses, not to mention relatives, police and lawyers involved. But the attempt to circulate the rumour seemed to show how many people there were ready to put the band down.

Even more disturbing was the spate of rumours, expressed in the rock press on both sides of the Atlantic, that somehow Jimmy's interest in the occult and Aleister Crowley had brought bad luck on the group. Strangely enough Rock magazine in its September issue asked on its

117

front cover 'Is there a curse on Led Zeppelin?' As a piece of sensational-
ism it could be dismissed, except that glossy colour magazines are
prepared well in advance of the publication date, and the article by one
Edward Stern seemed to have been written before the events of July 23
and 26. The writer proposed the theory that dabbling with the occult
had attracted negative forces which were trying to prevent the band
from reaching America.

'If we check the evidence and talk with the experts, it becomes
apparent that something truly 'supernatural' and eerie has attached
itself and gained a stronghold on the entire Led Zeppelin organisation.
This force has apparently been attempting to prevent Zeppelin from
reaching the shores of North America and performing before a legion of
loyal followers who have not had the privilege of seeing this super
group in two years.'

The article detailed Jimmy's interest in the paranormal, spells and
incantations. Another writer, Timothy Green Beckley, a rock critic and
student of the occult was also quoted as having studied Page's career.
'Certain developments may be a direct result of the rocker's attempt to
manipulate the forces of nature,' he claimed.

'It is important to remember that the vibes you send out, you will get
back. It's the law of Karma,' Beckley stated. 'When you play with fire
you are bound to get burned.' He thought it was possible Zeppelin had
called down 'nefarious influences' which had attempted to wreak havoc
on the group. He also thought it possible that 'another rock band' had
put a curse on Zeppelin. The article cited only the case of Robert's car
accident and illness, and nothing was said about the most recent cala-
mities. The article concluded: 'As Zeppelin travel in the United States,
Rock's readers can only hope nothing will prevent them from having a
successful tour. The curse hanging over their head may be so much
superstitious nonsense but for their own good it might just pay to be
extra cautious.'

The rumours and speculation only added to the misery felt by the
group. Jimmy was especially upset at all the talk of 'karma'. Back in
America there was considerable criticism of the Zeppelin entourage's
behaviour, and a report in Rolling Stone magazine gave a full account of
the attack on the security man, Jim Matzorkis. The headline was 'The
wrong goodbye: Led Zeppelin leaves America.'

Even at home it seemed the band were prone to endless troubles. In
September John Bonham broke two ribs in a car crash near his home.
The rumours about the band and its future continued afresh and Jimmy
began a series of interviews to attempt to allay fears and put the record
straight.

I met Jimmy in November 1977 and was shocked to see him tired,
strained, and visibly upset. His voice sank to a whisper, and he was

often barely audible as he talked in fits and starts. He firmly denied that Zeppelin would break up although after the death of Robert's son, there was obviously no thought of an early return to touring. This did not mean the group had ceased to exist or function.

He spoke about a new studio album, and a projected album of 'live' archive material to be assembled in chronological order. Jimmy spoke happily enough about these projects but when it came to the delicate subject of a curse on the band, or that the forces of Karma were at work, then he grew angry and upset.

'So much rubbish has been written about us recently. There was one thing about me joining The Stones and it even got to the point of them asking Mick Jagger if Robert was joining. I thought "This is getting really silly". There were rumours that the group was breaking up and all this sort of crap. For some reason I don't understand it just keeps going on. I thought it was a good idea to er, speak . . . ask me what you want.'

Was it true then as rumours suggested that Zeppelin would break up? 'No, definitely not. I've gotta say to you right now there are areas that are bloody touchy. You see I've never known a family to have such bad luck as Robert's, and it's really awful. . .' Here Jimmy seemed so upset his voice ground to a halt and he asked that as little be said about the tragedy as possible. Our conversation meandered on for another two hours during which he tried to emphasise the more positive aspects of the band's future work. He praised the new wave, and its energy, criticised bootleg albums as poor quality rip-offs, and mentioned the band's unfulfilled ambitions.

'We had a great plan to spend our non-British residence period (for tax reasons), soaking up the musical vibe in places like Morocco. We went there after Earls Court and spent quite a lot of time driving around there. We got turned back at the border on our way to the Sahara because there was a lot of mobilisation of troops going on.

But we heard a lot of local music and I was really influenced by them in tunes like *Achille's Last Stand*. The week of Robert's accident we had planned to go to Japan and Australia and then to work our way slowly through the East. We wanted to record in Bangkok, Delhi and Cairo and soak up the vibes as we had done in Morocco.

'At that time we had considered shelving the film *The Song Remains The Same* to film the forthcoming American tour. We had learnt a lot and wanted to re-do the film. But then, after Robert's accident, we had to fill the gap and go ahead with the film.'

Once again I mentioned the bad luck that dogged the group and Jimmy was greatly upset by the expression 'karma' that had been so freely put around.

'It's just the wrong term to ever use and how somebody could write that down, knowing the full facts about what happened I don't know. It

119

really shocks me. The whole concept of the band is of entertainment. I don't see any link between that and karma, and yet I've seen it written a few times about us, like "Yet another incident in Zeppelin's karma – John Paul Jones has broken his hand." It's nonsense, that was YEARS back. It's all crap.'

Recalling the mysterious informant who had waylaid me at a concert with tales of Zeppelin I wondered if the band had made enemies over the years, leading to deliberate rumour mongering. Jimmy pondered this in silence. 'No, I don't think so...', he said eventually. 'There was only the thing with Bill Graham and that was just a case of manhandling going on at the back of the stage, people getting pulled over the barriers and being given whacks. But I don't know anything about that. I didn't see what happened. I know that heavy vibe thing has surrounded us but it's more like ... well when Peter Grant did his scene in the film, it was really tongue in cheek. You couldn't find a gentler man, but people totally misunderstood him. And that thing about karma really bothers me. Wher₂'s the clue? I'm putting it to you to supply the answer. Why are they using that term? It's a horrible, tasteless thing to say. We shouldn't even discuss it. Just say that Jimmy Page is perplexed by the use of the word 'karma'. I just don't know what's going on.'

I felt so sorry for Jimmy and concerned at seeing the founder of Led Zeppelin under such pressure, I found it hard to make the suggestion that he was responsible for the 'karma' because of his dabbling in magic. And in any case, I didn't believe it for a moment. When the same questions came up, as they were bound to, in other interviews, Jimmy reacted in the same way, insisting that Led Zeppelin were all about entertaining people and bringing them pleasure. 'I don't see how the band would merit a karmic attack,' he told one reporter. 'All I have attempted to do is go out and have a good time and please people at the same time.

'I think it's just bad coincidence. Okay, one may say there's no such thing as coincidence, but I really feel that.' Asked if someone had put a curse on the band he replied: 'I can't account for the lunatic fringe.' As for the rumour that the band had killed someone during the Oakland incident, Jimmy said: 'That's nonsense! Listen, if we'd killed anybody, we'd be in bloody prison. It's ridiculous. It was just a civil case; if somebody hits you and you hit them back, it's self defence. It's just another thing that got blown up.

Bill Harry, their ex-publicist, who shared Jimmy's interest in the occult, as a subject worthy of academic study, discounted the idea of a 'curse'. Said Bill: 'There was no curse but luck did seem to go against them. On a trip to Sweden with them I talked to Jimmy about a book on witchcraft that I had read because I knew he had got into Aleister Crowley. I had studied the occult for a long time. There was no bad vibes about what Jimmy was into. His was like the search for the philosopher's stone. He wanted to heighten his consciousness. Other people tried to do it with drugs and LSD but Jimmy was trying to do it through mental awareness and was wrapped up in spells and was fascinated by Crowley as a character. Jimmy was a seeker of knowledge and like many people wanted to understand the meaning of life. He felt it couldn't just be a mundane existence. There had to be something more and some reason why we are here. The occult just means 'hidden knowledge' and it is not just about black magic.'

'What he liked about Crowley was that he was adept at sex magic. There were documented instances of Crowley being in the British Library with a beautiful girl. He'd just look at her and use his mental sex magic powers and the next thing he'd have her on one of the desks! That's what Jimmy was interested in. He wasn't interested in running naked through the woods with witches.

'At the time there was a lot of interest in England about reviving the old Wicca religion and witchcraft was being restarted. A lot of people confused this with study of the Occult and the kind of magic that interested Jimmy. He was seeking after truth. Crowley was called the most wicked man in England, but that was in England of the twenties and thirties. He was really a genius who didn't fit his time. People indulge in magic all the time, only they call it fantasy or day dreaming.

'People are limited by their circumstances and their own body, and have to make the best of it. You cannot be an ordinary person to make a success in life. You have to go over the top, go over the barricades. That's why Zeppelin had such an extraordinary lifestyle.'

Some thought that the four runic symbols on the fourth Led Zeppelin album had some mystical power, and Bill agreed this was probably true. 'The runes do have power. We are all living on one level of existence, but we have the power to change and alter things. Each day we have a certain amount of energy when we wake up. We can store it or expend it. We can use the power and the vibrations of the mind. A simple example. You can stare at the back of somebody's neck and they'll turn round and look at you.' Bill pointed out that like the runes, there was an ancient charm called Abraxas, composed of Greek letters which were alleged to have magical powers. The whole subject came to be of considerable interest to rock musicians in Britain and America.

'Everyone was seeking or looking for something. Rock musicians had the money and freedom to spend time thinking about what they were doing. It's why The Beatles took up meditation. It opened doors and helped provide inspiration for music and songs.

At the end of the disastrous year, Jimmy retreated into his home studio at Plumpton to write songs for the next studio LP and tinker with his 'live' material for a chronological album which never appeared.

121

Among the taped concerts at his disposal were The Royal Albert Hall 1969, Japan 1972, Southampton University 1971, Earls Court 1975 and several others. Unfortunately many bootleg tapes and LPs of these concerts, in particular the Earls Court shows, were already in circulation.

In February 1978 the criminal charges against Peter Grant, John Bonham, Richard Cole and John Bindon came to court in California. They received suspended sentences and probation, and fines of a few hundred dollars. They didn't have to appear in court, but if they had, then Bill Graham's men would have been able to present their civil lawsuits. Bill Graham thought they had got off lightly without learning any lessons. 'At worst in the next couple of years they'll just be careful that they're not seen.'

In May the band did the best thing they could in the circumstances. Quietly they got together for a month long series of rehearsals at Clearwell Castle near the Forest Of Dean, a place of tranquility and peace. It was the first time the group had made music together since the abrupt end of the American tour. Zeppelin fans at home began to wonder if the group would announce a tour. Instead there was a teasing succession of unpublicised secret gigs and jam sessions. Jimmy, still acting as main spokesman for the group, explained that the Clearwell sessions were 'basically a period of saying hello to each other musically once again. We hadn't played together for so long and Clearwell was the first actual playing we'd done for what seemed like an eternity, although it was only ten months.'

In July Robert made his first public appearances since the death of Karac. He sat in with bands in Worcestershire and sang with the mysterious Melvin Giganticus And The Turd Burglers at Wolverly Memorial Hall. He sang *I Got A Woman, Blue Suede Shoes* and other rock standards. Later, during a holiday in Ibiza in August, Robert went to the Club Amnesia, and jammed with Dr. Feelgood and Atlantic Records executive Phil Carson. Reported an astounded club manager, Stu Lyons: 'Robert looked in great shape and sounded fantastic.'

In September, the day after Zeppelin's tour manager Richard Cole got married, Robert sang with Dave Edmunds on stage at Birmingham Odeon. Then in October John Paul Jones and John Bonham took part in the Rockestra sessions organised by Paul McCartney at Abbey Road studios for Wings' *Back To The Egg* album.

Then at last Zeppelin began work on their next album, which for tax reasons had to be recorded out of the country, at the Polar Studios owned by Abba in Stockholm. 1978 had flashed by with very little activity from the band. But it seemed the wounds of 1977 had begun to heal, and many were delighted and relieved that Robert felt he could sing again and even contemplate the idea of playing concerts. Then came exciting news. The band would play a concert in England, at the Knebworth Festival in July. It would be the biggest in a series of massive concerts at the site, near Stevenage in Hertfordshire, organised by promoter Fred Bannister.

On July 24 and 25, 1979 the band played two surprise warm up concerts at the theatre in Copenhagen where the band had made their hesitant debut back in 1968. As tickets for the Knebworth show sold out, a second date was added. The first of the historic Knebworth shows was held on August 4, and the band were supported by Fairport Convention, Commander Cody, Chas and Dave, Southside Johnny and the Asbury Jukes and Todd Rundgren. The band played for three hours and did four encores.

On the second date, August 11, they were supported by Chas and Dave, Commander Cody, Southside Johnny, Todd Rundgren and Keith Richard's New Barbarians, a ramshackled ensemble who came on late, played badly and got ecstatic reviews in a 'quality' Sunday paper, while Zeppelin were called 'the worst band in the world'.

I went to the second Knebworth show, and it was the first time I'd seen the band since Earls Court. So much water had pased under the bridge, I could not but feel mixed emotions. I'd been to so many outdoor rock festivals over the previous sixteen years, I had lost count, although I guessed it amounted to around forty, ranging from three day all star marathons, to mudbaths in foreign fields. A kind of pop agrophobia – fear of festivals – was setting in.

But I couldn't miss a chance to see Zeppelin and in any case had to review it for a new, short-lived weekly paper called Musicians Only which I had recently joined. After what had seemed like a sizeable chunk of my life devoted to the cause of Melody Maker, I sought pastures new. The pastures turned out to be an arid desert of falling circulation and advertising revenue, followed by a sandstorm of strikes, lock outs and redundancy. But in September 1979 when I reviewed Led Zeppelin, the world still looked bright. It seemed a time for making fresh starts.

My first priority was to try and counteract some of the destructive criticism being levelled at the band of the 'Led Zeppelin – defunct dinosaurs' type. Not that I felt the band were above criticism. But they were being made victims of a kind of black propaganda war being waged by those who wished to deny the past and fashion the future according to their own lights. It was understandable, but unnecessary. Led Zeppelin posed no threat to German electronic pop, British New Romantics or post punk experimentalists, beyond the fact that they kept winning popularity polls and their records continued to sell in huge quantities. For young critics, attempting to champion new ideas, Zeppelin's very existence was an affront and all their efforts must necessari-

123

ly be scorned and vilified.

For example the Melody Maker proudly announced 'Exclusive Zep LP Review'. Editorial delight was confined to the acquisition of a copy of the album. The review by Chris Bohn, was full of crushing invective and sneering contempt and headed 'A Whole Lotta Bluff'. Rolling Stone described it as 'Sad Zep'. One British Sunday Paper described Zeppelin at Knebworth as 'The worst and noisiest group in the history of rock music'.

My own view was that the new album, *In Through The Out Door*, released on August 20, was a reflection of the band's desire to have fun, and not attempt to come on heavily in *Physical Graffiti* mode. In view of what they had been through, it was a wonder they were making records at all. Despite all the put downs and bad reviews, it went to Number One in both Britain and America. It was Number One in the US for seven weeks and sold around four million copies – not bad for redundant dinosaurs, who had 'squeezed their lemons dry a long time ago'. To show there was no hard feelings, the band attended the Melody Maker's annual pop poll awards where they had won most of the categories. Desperate attempts were later made to prevent popular rock groups from winning the awards by altering the categories.

In my review of Knebworth I wrote: 'In view of the excessive tripe written about Led Zeppelin at Knebworth it is a matter of some urgency that fans who could not be present be reassured. The band were excellent, their performance superb. The cacophony of orchestrated criticism which followed. . . . was laughable.'

But I noted that the audience reaction from the mainly young fans, newcomers to Zeppelin, was strangely subdued compared to the explosive enthusiasm I recalled from their early days.

Even the audience at the last of the two Knebworth's took a helluva lot of coaxing into action. Perhaps they had been bored into the ground by the long wait which the New Barbarians shamelessly perpetrated before their set, and the musical tedium which followed. At any rate, Robert Plant – bravely returning to rock after the shattering blows of the past – seemed perplexed at the lack of reaction. I remembered the days when there was an electrifying rapport between Zeppelin and their audience. You could almost hear a pin drop in the darkness at Knebworth as 100,000 stood in silence during some of the breaks and quieter songs. They seemed curiously slow in responding to Robert's cajoling.

But it occurred to me this was the awkwardness of strangers at the party, and a not a reflection on the group's performance.

It had been ten years since Fred Bannister had promoted the Bath Festival where Zeppelin had made their British breakthrough and most of the audience at Knebworth had never seen them before. I too wondered if Zeppelin could still evoke their old cataclysmic power. 'Within seconds of their launching into action it was obvious that not only had Zeppelin retained their musical grip but had reached a new state of perfection in their art. In the old days Zeppelin gigs were often disjointed, raw and not always well paced. Now the band have polished and honed their ideas and each individual's contribution is edited and yet showcased to greater effect.'

I noted that John Paul Jones' piano work had blossomed and he was now featured as a 'rhapsodic but tasteful soloist alongside the pungent attack of Jimmy's guitar.' John Bonham's drum solo was cut out entirely, but the monumental power and precision of his accompaniment was a wonder itself.

'Robert's voice, that most sensual and emotional instrument, had lost none of its spine tingling vibrancy and was especially appreciated on the slow blues.' The band played *Stairway To Heaven*, *No Quarter* and *Trampled Underfoot* and was greeted with a roar of applause. I pointed out that the band could still defeat all opposition on their home ground and suggested that the gale of indifference that blew from many critics would eventually sap their morale. 'I would not blame them if they never played Britain again.' Of course, they never did.

Just over a year after the triumphant return at Knebworth, the band was shattered by the sudden death of John Bonham. And following a period of mourning and speculation came the news. Led Zeppelin would not find a replacement drummer. They would sooner disband. The Zeppelin saga, one of the most extraordinary in the thirty year history of rock, was at an end.

NINE

CODA

'It's been quite good,' was Robert Plant's guarded comment at the end of the Knebworth concerts. Even so there was a spirit of optimism abroad during the winter of 1979. Polls around the world showed Zeppelin still one of the world's most popular bands. Almost single-handed the group had managed to reverse the great slump in the American record business. The arrival of *In Through The Out Door* in August 1979 had, according to Atlantic Records general manager Dave Glen, 'Given the whole industry a shot in the arm.'

Within four days of release, Atlantic received an additional 900,000 orders for the Zeppelin LP and by the end of September, had shipped three million copies. There was also heavy demand for previous Zeppelin albums and Atlantic had to ship out a further million copies. The result was all nine Zep albums occupied places in the Billboard Top 200 chart during the last week of October.

In Through The Out Door stayed in the American chart at Number One for seven weeks and in the Top Twenty for six months. Sales were not so good at home. The LP was Number One for two weeks only in the Music Week chart. But it was still the seventh Zeppelin album to enter the chart at Number One in the first week of release. And it went gold from U.K. sales by the end of 1979.

Under pressure from radio stations and record companies, Zeppelin released their first American single in three and a half years when Swan

126

Song put out *Fool In The Rain* and *Hot Dog* from the album just before Christmas. It got into the U.S. Top Twenty but there was no inclination by the group to issue singles anywhere else.

There was sporadic Zeppelin activity when Robert, John Paul and Bonzo went to the Wings' Kampuchea Benefit concert at the Odeon Hammersmith, London on December 29. Robert sat in with Dave Edmund's Rockpile and the rest joined Paul McCartney's all-star Rockestra group. Robert made another quick appearance with Rockpile in February 1980 when the band played at Birmingham Top Rank which fuelled speculation that Robert was looking for other musicians to work with on a solo project.

In April the band began rehearsing at the Rainbow Theatre in London for a full European tour. The following month rehearsals were switched to the New Victoria Theatre while the tour dates were constantly revised. Eventually it was announced the band would play fourteen dates in Germany, Holland, Belguim and Switzerland. As Bonzo celebrated his thirty-second birthday, the band carried on rehearsals at Shepperton Studios. At the same time it was announced that Jimmy intended to buy Michael Caine's old home in Windsor for around £900,000.

The 'Over Europe 80' tour began in Dortmund on June 17 followed by dates at Cologne (18), Brussels (20), Rotterdam (21), Bremen (23), Vienna (26), and Nuremberg (27). Unfortunately the latter show was cancelled after only three numbers when Bonham collapsed from physical exhaustion.

He recovered in time for the rest of the dates including Zurich (29), Frankfurt (30), Mannheim (July 2 and 3), Munich (5), and Berlin (7). The band was in high humour throughout the dates and dressed in their usual odd mixture of styles and fashions, with Jimmy in a baggy suit and white scarf and Robert in his inevitable blue jeans and a green tee shirt. They opened each show with the old Yardbirds number *Train Kept A Rollin'*, and the programme usually included *Nobody's Fault But Mine, Black Dog, In The Evening, The Rain Song, Hot Dog, Trampled Underfoot*, the bluesy *Since I've Been Loving You, Achilles Last Stand*, with a spot of duck walking from Jimmy, *White Summer, Black Mountain Side, Kashmir, Stairway To Heaven, Rock And Roll*, and finally *Whole Lotta Love*.

In Munich there was a surprise guest spot when an extra drum kit was set up and Bad Company drummer Simon Kirke played alongside Bonzo during *Whole Lotta Love*. In Frankfurt, Zeppelin's honorary bass player, Phil Carson, sat in on *Money*.

Simon Kirke thoroughly enjoyed his moment of glory with Zeppelin. It happened at the Munich Olympia Halle and recalled Simon: 'Bonzo and I did a duet. We did *Whole Lotta Love* and we had two kits up there.

127

Peter Grant has got a tape of it and one day it might even come out. It was all arranged well before hand but it was supposed to be secret. Bonzo said "I'll get it fooking organised." He phoned all the instrument dealers in Munich and said "I want a fooking drum kit sent down, right away."

'Well you know it's quite a complex arrangement to *Whole Lotta Love*. It was a twelve minute piece. So Bonzo says to me, banging on his knees, "Right we do this, got that? Right, then Pagey takes over, bomp, bomp got that? Fooking great." And it was all done on the knees in the hotel room before we went on stage. I dunno how, but I got through to the end. The only thing that upset me was I found all the cymbals were the wrong way round. But hearing those opening notes was the heaviest thing I've ever heard. And then of course ... he died just a month or so later. And yet John was fine when I saw him.

'In fact the LAST time I saw him he was packing up little dolls he had collected from every country for his daughter Zoe. So this image of the wild man eating maids for breakfast was wiped out. He was wrapping up all these little dolls ... "One from Austria, one from Switzerland..." And he was such a tidy man. He was in the tailoring trade once and his suits were always immaculate.'

Many British fans flocked to Germany to see the band on what would prove to be their last tour. Among them was Dave Lewis, editor of the Zeppelin fan magazine Tight But Loose, in which he reported on the concerts. Wrote Lewis: 'Let me tell you about the rejuvenation this band has obviously undergone ... I'd say Zeppelin have gone full circle. In every aspect of their performance it was almost back to the roots. From the old Yardbirds number up to the twelve-year-old classic *Whole Lotta Love* and everything in between ... they've still got it and they still care.'

John Bonham told Lewis after the shows: 'Overall everyone has been dead chuffed with the way the tour's gone. There were so many things that could have gone wrong. It was a bit of a gamble this one, but it's worked really well. We wanna keep working. There's lots of possibilities and of course we want to do England. It's down to a management decision really and we will have to talk about that when we get back.'

On their return to Britain it was announced that Zeppelin would do their first American tour since 1977, with nineteen dates, starting in Montreal, Canada on October 17. Immediately queues began to form at North American box offices as fans eagerly anticipated the return of the legends.

In September the band began rehearsals at Jimmy's new home in Windsor. It was then that tragedy struck once more. I was in Amsterdam covering a concert by a band called Sad Cafe. On the morning of Friday 26 September 1980 I had been trying to dial London about twenty times to phone home my flight's arrival time. When I finally got through I was told that John Bonham had died. There had been no English papers in Amsterdam that morning due to a blanket of fog. I was shocked at the news, especially as John Bonham, of all the stars of rock, seemed the steadiest, most durable of people, with so much to live for.

Then the details came through as I received phone calls from national newspapers and radio stations asking for comment on the tragedy. John had been found dead at Jimmy Page's new home, Old Mill House, Windsor, on September 25. His body was found in bed by John Paul Jones. Bonzo had been drinking heavily before and during rehearsals the previous day and had been put to bed by Jimmy's personal assistant, Rick Hobbs. Police were called to the house, but there were no suspicious circumstances.

An inquest was held on October 8 and it was revealed that John had died from inhaling his own vomit during his sleep, the same fate that had befallen Jimi Hendrix. It was also two years to the month since the death of Bonham's drumming pal Keith Moon. It seemed that John had started a lunchtime drinking session at a pub near his home in Cutnall Green, then carried on drinking until midnight. He had consumed something like forty measures of vodka during his twelve hour session. He fell asleep on a sofa and was put to bed and laid on his side with pillows for support.

When it was realised something was wrong some hours later, an ambulance was called but John was already dead. A verdict of accidental death was recorded. Friends told how John had been very tense and nervous about the band's return to America where there had been such bad feeling on their last trip.

The group were shattered by the death of their friend, and all plans for touring were immediately cancelled. John's funeral took place at Rushock Parish church in Worcestershire on October 10. At a cremation ceremony many of his friends and musicians attended, including Roy Wood, Denny Laine, Bev Bevan and Jeff Lynne. Tributes came pouring in from the rock world, with particularly high praise from his fellow drummers.

Said Simon Kirke: 'I felt very privileged to have known Bonzo. We were roughly the same age, and we were each other's fans. He was my all-time favourite drummer, and he was the best. There was no one within a mile of Bonzo.'

Said Dave Lewis in a tribute in Tight But Loose: 'Those who were close to him will know the real John Bonham. Behind all the exaggerated rock 'n' roll lunacy that comes with their lifestyle he was a big hearted, warm, caring family man. A very special character indeed. And it goes without saying he was a drummer of extraordinary talent who as part of Led Zeppelin, gave immense pleasure to millions the world over.'

129

Other tributes came from Carmine Appice, Phil Collins, Cozy Powell and Carl Palmer. And soon there were rumours that Bonham would be replaced, in the same way Kenny Jones took Keith Moon's place in The Who. Among those suggested as a contender was Carmine Appice, the American drummer who came to fame with Vanilla Fudge and Jeff Beck, and had been something of an inspiration to John. Said Carmine: 'I heard rumours that I'd be asked to join Zeppelin and felt bad about it. He always treated me with a lot of respect. He was one of the boys and one of the best.'

It had not been so long since I enjoyed an evening's drink with John, at the same pub where he began his ill-fated session. I had gone to see him for an interview at his farm, back in June 1975. It gave me a chance to get to known John the farmer, stock breeder and family man, as well as Bonzo the world's heaviest drummer. The day before I saw him his wife Pat had just given birth to a baby daughter Zoe and there was cause for celebration. Although he had just been banned from driving for six months, he was feeling content and satisfied. He poured out his ideas, opinions and thoughts in tones that brooked no argument, and yet he had a fearless quality which commanded respect. He looked you straight in the eye with twinkling good humour. I recalled the long hours of conversation in the deserted farmhouse out in the Worcester-shire countryside.

His farm and its modern brick farmhouse seemed like the ponderosa in the TV series *Bonanza*, with its ranchstyle nameboard swinging at the head of a long straight drive way. I asked John if he had always intended to go into farming. 'Never, I was never into farming at all. I wasn't even looking for a farm, just a house with some land. But when I saw this place, something clicked and I bought it back in 1972.'

Robert Plant lived just a few miles away on another farm, surrounded by goats, which said John 'Eat everything, old boots, you name it!' He showed me the hundred acres of land surrounding his house, on which cattle and sheep safely grazed. The view was beautiful, if somewhat spoilt by a line of new electricity pylons.

Despite the intensive agricultural activity, there was no mistaking that the farmer was also a rock 'n' roller. In a barn called 'the hot car shop' John had stored a collection of flashy cars. They included a 150 mph American showcar, with wide wheels and misshapen body, a 1967 Corvette with a seven litre engine, and a 1954 two door Ford with a secret eight litre engine. Said John proudly: 'You get guys coming past in a sports car who think it's an old banger, until I put my foot down.'

John had once bought a Rolls Royce early in his career and soon learned such a status symbol could be a liability. 'It was a white one. I went to a wedding in Birmingham. When I came out it looked like a bomb had hit it. All these skinheads had jumped on it. They kicked in

130

the windscreen, smashed everything. If it had been any other car, they would have left it alone.'

Inside the house John talked to me about his early days and drumming career. He explained that the farmhouse used to be a three bedroom affair which had been extended and improved by himself. 'My father did all the wood panelling and I did a lot of the work with my brother and sub-contractors. When I left school I went into the trade with my dad. He had a building business, and I liked it.'

I drove John to the local pub in the evening, and the conversation ranged over a variety of topics, from farming to drumming. 'Not everybody likes or understands a drum solo,' he reflected. 'So I like to bring in effects and sounds to keep their interest, like 'phasing' on pedal tympani. I've been doing a hand drum solo for a long time, before I joined Led Zeppelin. I remember playing a solo on *Caravan* when I was sixteen. Sometimes you can chunck out of your knuckles on the hi-hat or you can catch your hand on the tension rods. I try to play something different every night on my solo, but the basic plan is the same, from sticks to hands, and then the tymps and the final build up. It would be really boring to play on the same kit all the time. I usually play for twenty minutes and the longest I've ever done was just under thirty. It's a long time but when I'm playing it seems to fly by.

'Sometimes you come up against a blank and you think "How am I going to get out of this one?" Or sometimes you go into a fill and you know halfway through it's going to be disastrous. There have been times when I've blundered and got the dreaded look from the lads. But that's a good sign. It shows you are attempting something you've not tried before.'

He admitted that despite his confident manner he suffered from doubt and worry just before every concert. The thoughts of having to keep up the excitement and drive for two to three hours a night on the road, sometimes bought on a sort of panic attack. It wasn't so much the playing as the waiting.'

'I've got worse – terrible bad nerves all the time. Once we start into *Rock And Roll* I'm fine. I just can't stand sitting around, and I worry about playing badly and if I do then I'm really pissed off. If I play well, I feel fine. Everybody in the band is the same and each has some little thing they do before we go on, like pacing about or lighting a cigarette. It's worse at festivals.'

'You might have to sit around for a whole day and you daren't drink because you'll get tired out and blow it. So you sit drinking tea in a caravan with everybody saying "far out man".'

Despite the pleasure building up his home and farming business gave him, John always yearned to play. He told me that night in the pub drinking pints of local bitter: 'I wish there were some more live bands

131

around here I could have a blow with. There's nowhere for them to play now, it's all discos. God, I hate those places, all those flashing lights. It's all right if you're out for a night on the tiles. But I like to hear a good live group. You gotta remember – they're the backbone of the business.'

John was doing his best for the business by training his son Jason to be a drummer. He was then nine-years-old and I met him in his cub uniform bashing away on a junior drum kit set up in front of his dad's juke box. There he pounded away to Gary Glitter records. 'You can't teach him anything,' John warned me as we watched Jason attacking his kit. 'He's got a terrible temper.' Years later I saw Jason the teenager, playing with a real live rock band, Air Race, and showing he had indeed learned a lot from his dad, and had become an excellent drummer in his own right.

Speculation about the future of Zeppelin continued to grow throughout the remaining months of 1980. Then in December a London evening paper ran a story suggesting that Bonham's place was about to be filled and the band would start touring again.

On December 4 Swan Song put out a statement to news agencies which said: 'We wish it to be known that the loss of our dear friend and the deep sense of undivided harmony felt by ourselves and our manager, have led us to decide that we could not continue as we were.'

Their record company would accept no further calls or make any further comment. Later Jimmy Page explained that he couldn't have carried on with Led Zeppelin, playing the same old numbers, without John Bonham on drums. 'It would have been an insult' he said firmly.

After a period of respectful silence, yet more rumours began to suggest the possibility of the old Zeppelin crew forming a band with ex-members of Yes. This came to nothing, although a supergroup called Asia did emerge, and the band Cinema, which might have included Jimmy Page, reformed as Yes, without him.

It was plain that Jimmy and Robert Plant would pursue separate solo careers, John Paul Jones would retire into the Surrey countryside and there would be no Zeppelin reunion. Jimmy made the first move towards tangible activity, writing the music for the thriller film, directed by his neighbour Michael Winner, called *Death Wish II*, which was released as a soundtrack album. And in March 1981 he made a surprise appearance with his old Yardbirds' colleague Jeff Beck, in a show at Hammersmith Odeon.

Robert began jamming with friends and turned up on BBC TV's *Pop Quiz* show as a contestant, surprising fans by sporting a short haircut and looking older and subdued. He was keen to do interviews, in which he said little about the past, and determined to move forward and find a successful and valid role in the Eighties. In a sense he was picking up the pieces of his own career as a singer and composer, which he had left behind to join forces with Zeppelin.

With a new guitar partner, Robbie Blunt, he put together the songs for his first album *Pictures At Eleven* released in 1982 and *The Principles Of Moments* which came out in 1983. The same year he began a British and American tour, backed by such top ranking musicians as Phil Collins, Robbie Blunt and Cozy Powell. On his first album the music was fairly straightforward, but he began to experiment on the second with pieces like *Big Log* and *In The Mood*.

Robert commented on his new musical direction: 'The goal really is to keep stretching. It was the same with Zeppelin and it's the same with me now.' Robert had begun his return to work after the demise of Zeppelin with a band called The Honeydrippers. They were local musicians and he began singing with them in unpublicised performances from February 1981.

'It was extremely hard for me to even consider working with other people', he told reporter Steve Gett. 'I didn't want to play with anyone initially and then the Honeydrippers sort of got me at it again. Robbie Blunt and I played in the Honeydrippers for quite a while, playing out our fantasies with an R&B horn section. It was enjoyable and we went around the country appearing in small clubs. But gradually we began to realise the limitations as things got a bit repetitious. It wasn't a serious thing and we didn't want to play twelve-bar blues for ever. But it was great fun to go out and do it without any of the usual pressures.'

During this period of unpressured jamming, Robert and Robbie also began writing material together and in September 1981 began work on the first album at Rockfield Studio. The musicians Robert used included bassist Paul Martinez, keyboard player Jezz Woodroffe and drummer Cozy Powell. Cozy cut two of the tracks on the album and Phil Collins did the rest. The album was released to critical acclaim and did well in the charts but Robert steered clear of touring until he had enough songs of his own to take out in front of the public. He wasn't going to come back singing old Led Zeppelin hits. 'I love the numbers' he told Steve, 'but I ain't gonna play Zeppelin songs without Zeppelin.'

The same line-up, with Barriemore Barlowe instead of Cozy Powell on some tracks, recorded *The Principle Of Moments* back at Rockfield Studios, in Monmouth, during July 1982. Robert looked forward to his tour which was a considerable success and didn't seem to mind being the first of the old Zeppelins to go out alone. 'I think it's a great challenge. There's nothing tough about it. I don't think I can find anything as tough as I've already had.'

Robert made a considerable impression with his work as a producer and composer and he continued to establish his independence and sense of purpose by releasing his second LP on his own Es Paranza label. And in late August of 1983 Robert began his first concert work as a solo artist with a six week tour of America.

During Robert's British dates, Jimmy Page appeared on stage at a show in Bristol on December 13 and played *Little Sister*. John Paul Jones sat in on bass during another show, while Jason Bonham, now a star of Air Race, played drum on *Burning Down One Side* at Birmingham Odeon on December 24.

The fans tended to accept Robert's new songs and didn't cry out too much for old Zeppelin hits. Said one review: 'From the high spirits throughout the crowd it was obvious that Plant remains as much beloved on his own as he was with Zeppelin. No one I've seen on tour over the past year drew such a consistently excited response.'

Robert continued to refuse to perform any old Zeppelin numbers and said: 'I don't think it would be fair to anybody that I'm playing with now if they had to go through the motions of something that they hadn't been responsible for recording in the first place, and more so, hadn't been responsible for writing.'

After two successful solo albums charted around the world, Robert said: 'I'm finally coming to terms with a new role in a new game.'

Meanwhile the tenth Led Zeppelin LP *Coda* consisting of a mix of tracks from 1969 to 1978 produced by Jimmy Page was released in November 1982. And in October Swan Song Records released Robert's *Burning Down One Side* as a single cut from *Pictures At Eleven*. *Big Log* was also released as a single from his second album in 1983.

Jimmy Page appeared at various concerts and club gigs over the next couple of years, with a shorter hair style and a suit, perhaps taking his cue from Eric Clapton who had also smartened up his appearance as middle age approached. Despite talk of a split between Robert and Jimmy, the pair remained firm friends; when Robert completed his first solo album he took it to Jimmy to hear first. The pair jammed with Foreigner in Munich in 1982.

The following year Jimmy appeared in charity concerts at London's Royal Albert Hall to raise funds for research into the wasting disease, multiple sclerosis, which had struck down Ronnie Lane, the bass player with The Small Faces and later with Rod Stewart and The Faces. Ronnie was a popular figure in the rock community and many musicians came together at his behest for two emotional concerts which eventually grew into eight nights at Madison Square Garden in New York, followed by concerts in Dallas and San Francisco.

I went to see the concert at the Royal Albert Hall on September 21, 1983. The line-up included Jimmy, Jeff Beck, Eric Clapton, Steve Winwood and Simon Phillips, together with Bill Wyman, Charlie Watts and Andy Fairweather Low. The concert was attended by the Prince and Princess of Wales and it was a unique opportunity to see together all the artists I had so admired during the Sixties – and Seventies. The fact they

134

played so well, made it all the more worthwhile.

Undoubtedly the most remarkable moment was when Jimmy Page came out to play alone some guitar improvisations which turned into a most moving version of *Stairway To Heaven*. It seemed as if Page was crying through his guitar. There were certainly many memories aroused by the sight of Jimmy prowling around the stage, cigarette between his lips, as he played, first hesitantly and then with increasing power and passion. Later Jimmy joined a classic line-up – Eric, Jeff and Page, the stalwarts of the old Yardbirds in line abreast, riffing together. It was over all too soon.

Apart from these unique appearances, Jimmy spent his time at his own Sol Studios rehearsing and recording, and finding relaxation in such innocent pursuits as playing snooker and taking an interest in cricket. He remained fascinated by old bootleg albums of Led Zeppelin.

Robert moved to London after years in the country and began to build an increasingly high profile. He too played a charity gig in aid of the Prince's Trust at the Dominion Theatre, London in July 1982. The show was featured on video tape and included Phil Collins, Pete Townshend, Midge Ure, Mick Karn, Robbie Blunt, Madness, Peter Tosh and Ian Anderson. The 'Rock Gala' was a great success and Robert sang *Worse Than Detroit*.

In June 1984 Jimmy Page and his old friend and hero, folk singer and guitarist Roy Harper, began recording together to produce an album, and they began playing gigs with a band. At first Jimmy played under the name of James McGregor, working as a duo with Roy under great secrecy. They performed at the May Tree Fair, at the Medieval Hall, Thetford, and before that played with keyboardist Nick Green and a drum machine at the St. Ives Hotel, a folk room in Blackpool.

Next they planned to play at the prestigious Cambridge Folk Festival, a long running affair, billed as The McGregors. But then Jimmy and Roy decided to go the whole hog and reveal their colours, while announcing that an album was imminent.

They played two spots at the Festival on Saturday, July 28, 1984 with a full band in the afternoon on the main outdoor stage and then a more intimate affair under canvas later that evening. The band included Nick Green (keyboards), Tony Franklin (bass) and Steve Broughton on drums, all described as 'Roy's mates from Blackpool'.

It was a beautiful, hot sunny day, perfect for unveiling Harper and Page in a relaxed atmosphere. They wanted nothing to do with the music press and already Roy had been incensed by some sneering remarks made about their project. 'I'll get my revenge' he said. 'The fact is our age doesn't matter. We may have been playing for a long time but we still have a lot of music and new ideas to offer.'

When I arrived at the festival I found Roy sitting in his own tent,

135

somewhat nervously awaiting the arrival of Jimmy from a local hotel. The band were due on stage in about half an hour. 'I've got to get the band together now, and Jimmy hasn't turned up yet,' he smiled. But there was nothing to worry about.

I went backstage and suddenly a figure dashed across through the gloom of a cavernous marquee. 'Hello Welchy – you old wanker.' This cheery greeting came from James Patrick Page, clad in a gleaming white suit and long scarf.

Jimmy was delighted at being back at work and he busied himself tuning up guitars reverently laid out on the grass. There wasn't much time for chat. 'This is our first gig with the band,' said Jimmy. 'It's a bit funny playing in the afternoon.'

It was a master stroke of Jimmy to play such an event, despite the bright sunshine glaring into his eyes. And much credit was due to Roy in encouraging him. If he had tried to launch a powerhouse heavy metal band into something like the Reading Festival, he would have to run the gauntlet of fans screaming and hurling beer cans at each other, and critics hurling barbed epithets. There would have been comparisons with Led Zeppelin, howls of rage and disappointment if he didn't play *Dazed And Confused*. Here, at Cambridge, the fans obediently obeyed the compere's instructions to sit down. 'And you couldn't do that at Reading,' said the MC Alex Atterson, a Scot who was greatly amused by the cries of 'Hey Jimmy!'

Apart from the shouts of a few loyal Zeppelin fans who had infiltrated the folk lovers, the mood was warm, receptive and understanding. Nobody made impossible requests for old Zep numbers and Roy was able to sing his passionate songs without interruption.

Nevertheless there was tension and an atmosphere of expectancy as the band wandered into view. There was much tuning up, squeaks of feedback and fiddling about with equipment. Roy Harper proved he is still a man capable of mesmerising audiences with his humour and gestures. 'Shut up peasants!' was his opening remark.

The organisers had betrayed fears that fans would somehow rush the stage the minute Jimmy appeared, and attempts were made to clear the press enclosure. Their fears were groundless. All sat back in the sunshine and enjoyed the rolling, tumbling music that developed. Deceptively languid, it built to a series of climaxes throughout an hour long set.

Fans chattered excitedly as the band took up positions. 'Is he going to do any Zep stuff?' 'I dunno, I asked him to do *Achilles Last Stand* when I went backstage.' 'Well a bit of the *Bron-Y-Aur Stomp* would go down a treat.'

Jimmy Page was the last to come on stage, his white scarf trailing and a cigarette dangling from his lips. The audience waited on tenterhooks.

What on earth was he going to play? A few tentative notes came from Roy's guitar and the band gradually joined in. Roy and the bass player sang, and it was all 'tight but loose' as Jimmy might say. They played a tune called *Referendum* and Jimmy seemed to be having trouble with his foot switch. A roadie rushed in to sort it out. Then they played *Elizabeth*, described as a 'song for peace', another item from the Page & Harper LP.

Page's guitar wasn't loud enough, but when it came through he began to build up layers of notes in his own unique, indefinable way. His face was consumed in saturnine ecstacy, a picture of cat-like contentment. It was strange. As I watched and listened, a heavy riff came through that sounded not unlike The Kinks in their heyday. Suddenly time rolled in reverse. Not to Jimmy's session days, but back even further, to the young kid with Neil Christian and the Crusaders. I was sure this was how he looked and sounded in that legendary band. The vision of Page as a kid playing his first gig, somehow intruded, like a cinematic flashback.

Sometimes the two guitarists play to unison, Roy playing a lot of fine atmospheric stuff, to match Jimmy's faster finger. It all started to get heavy. Roy broke a string. Jimmy threw away his cigarette and his guitar began to howl. The cheers came and the band wanted to play an encore. But now time was running out. The compere ushered them off stage. Said Roy later: 'We had a couple more songs up our sleeves.' What had Jimmy thought of the gig: 'Well it was okay, but I could not hear the guitar very well.' It seemed there had been problems, including poor on-stage monitoring. But as the apologetic compere told the pair: 'It was a smashing set. I wish we'd had time for more.'

In that long hot summer of 1984 there were signs of activity from most of the members of the old band. Young Jason Bonham, looking astoundingly like his dad, was busy building up the reputation of his band Air Race, and playing drums with enormous power in the family tradition. There was even talk of Robert and Jimmy getting together again for a project, while Page was heavily involved in rehearsing his own new band – working title The Mac.

Whatever the future then held for the men who had created Led Zeppelin, it was heartening to know they still had a common aim and driving need. They had enjoyed all the fame, money and success. But they still needed to make a whole lot more music.

TEN

THE ZEPPELIN TREASURE HUNT

Led Zeppelin produced nine albums between 1969 and 1979. *Coda*, their tenth was produced by Jimmy Page and released after the group's demise. The band always maintained high standards, although there was a discernible pattern to their output.

They began at a peak with their first two albums and curved down to *Houses Of The Holy* in 1973. They peaked again with the critically acclaimed *Physical Graffiti* in 1974 and with *In Through The Out Door* in 1979. Doubtless there would have been many more such peaks had the band survived. And the changing pattern in their quality depends on personal viewpoints. The band expressed pride in all their albums and pointed out that each had something to offer. Robert, for example, was particularly fond of *Houses Of The Holy*.

Zeppelin constantly explored new ideas which were not always immediately to the liking of their audience. But they could not atrophy. The Zeppelin of *Whole Lotta Love* was so popular, and so binding an image, they could have gone on reproducing such basic riffs ad infinitum. Indeed they kept old favourites in their stage act, but because they were good and deserved to be played. On album they could cast their net wider. The bulk of their later albums represents a band on a mission, to find within themselves more music, to try new things.

From first to last, however, they retained the Zeppelin sound, and were rarely influenced by external pop influences, however much they

138

shook up everybody else. Zeppelin's music was a combination of stubborn resolve and personal passions. The instrumental prowess and songwriting skill was in a sense almost incidental, to be taken as read. The technique at their command enabled the creative juices to flow.

There was a shift of emphasis over the years. Their folk and blues roots showed more in their early work. Later they seemed to yearn for the simplicity of urban rock 'n' roll and even country music. Their more obvious excursions into ethnic forms, away from the stage fare of basic rock, was usually in the nature of a celebration, given fullest expression on *Fool In The Rain*.

The band left a considerable heritage of music on record for future generations to dissect, argue over and enjoy. The bootleg albums and tapes serve as historical footnotes to the legitimate albums. They fill in gaps in the history, and show the band at work, warts and all. Those who saw Zeppelin in their early days cannot fail to be moved on hearing, for example, the double bootleg *Live At The Lyceum In London*, recorded in October 1969 and released on a German label. The sound quality was appalling and the drums inaudible during the opening moments of the classic *Good Times, Bad Times*. But to hear Jimmy's guitar intro to *I Can't Quit You*, followed by Robert's extended cry from the heart, was worth it all. This was the stuff which so thrilled fans and converted them in droves.

Through such time machine records we can rediscover Zeppelin as a raw, rough but still electrifying experience. During the course of this long lost concert, Robert Plant talked about the 'new' album *Led Zeppelin II* and introduced a track from it, *Heartbreaker*, and apologised for the delays in its release. The various songs were all performed without particular regard for the official album versions which have since become so familiar. They cut short famous riffs, extended others and Jimmy allowed himself a great deal of space for fast and furious guitar solos, tending to leave Bonzo and John Paul Jones behind in the process. Later they would learn to structure their numbers more cohesively.

Zeppelin in 1969 were still very much a British blues band, with polite applause between numbers, and space for Robert to make club style announcements about the origins of tunes. He explained that *You Shook Me* came from an old Muddy Waters EP in his collection. So much for the theory that Zep never acknowledged their debt to past bluesmen.

Within a few years, as they roamed around the world, they became much more of a show band, with a scheduled programme and solos well placed for maximum effect at the right time. Even so, they were still prone to unexpected changes as a Japanese bootleg from a Tokyo concert showed. John Bonham staged a rebellion and arrived late for his drum solo as an anguished Robert explained. Running slow due to faulty recording, this was one bootleg that didn't do the band any

139

favours.

Fans armed with pocket tape recorders managed to capture most of the band's historic concerts like Earls Court 1975, which can be heard on record and audio cassettes running into three volumes of material. Better recorded than the early efforts, nevertheless there is a limit to how much even the most dedicated fan wants to hear by his favourite group. The bootlegs bring back memories and fulfil a need to hear the whole story, but the official albums give the most satisfaction, and value for money.

For example, the first album *Led Zeppelin* was superb, essentially a 'live' performance, albeit made in a studio. The wild cascade of notes in the middle of *You Shook Me* was just one of a series of electrifying outbursts of spontaneous creation that sounds just as exciting today as it did back in 1969.

Another piece of magic on this pioneering album was the famed 'grand entry' into *Dazed And Confused*, with sombre walking bass and howling response from the guitar to Robert Plant's anguished vocal. These were the songs that captured the spirit of a brave new band finding its feet, and discovering each other's talents and skills. A telling moment was the chuckle, detectable through headphones, when Robert performs a particularly tricky piece of vocal gymnastics in unison with the guitar during *You Shook Me*.

The whole band was spurred on by John Bonham's Wagnerian drumming and they reached a frantic peak during the double tempo section of *Dazed And Confused*, one of the greatest rock arrangements on record. Side one alone packed in more original music than appeared on all the thousands of rock albums subsequently released during the next decade.

It was as if all the expertise and pent up enthusiasm of John Paul Jones and Jimmy Page, from their years of stifling session work had been released and fuelled by the arrival of the 'new boys' Robert and Bonzo. All the Zeppelin trademarks, including Jimmy's erotic guitar accompaniment to Robert's equally sexy screams, were aired on an album that launched not just a band, but a new age of rock 'n' roll.

It was obvious from the start that Zeppelin were much more than a louder, faster blues band, and the phrase 'heavy metal' just didn't do them justice. It ignores the subtleties of *Black Mountain Side* and the way this piece faded in from *Your Time Is Gonna Come*, the eerie flavour heightened by the use of tabla drums and sitar effects.

A sudden jump into *Communication Breakdown* was inspired production, although on this early version of the tune, the distortion on Robert's vocal track was unnecessary.

It celebrated the birth of the band but this was no breakdown. It was sheer communication, and there was more to come with the astounding

140

I Can't Quit You Baby, credited to Willie Dixon. The mood was pure Zeppelin though, and if there were any external influences they came more from the Les Paul guitar style used in Jimmy's backing to Robert's shout.

There was a jazz feeling too in the way John Bonham swung on his big ride cymbals behind Jimmy's solos, and in the panther like beat to *How Many More Times*. Here Robert fenced lightly with the storming wall of riffs before unleashing his full petulant fury.

Led Zeppelin II (1969) wasn't just a good follow up, it was a great leap forward, while developing the same sort of excitement and attack eager fans had quickly come to expect. So often a new band with great promise and a big build up stumbles when it comes to the second album. Zeppelin just steamed into *II* with all guns blazing. There was even another catchy, commercial and decidedly heavy riff to follow up *Communication Breakdown*. This time it was the sonorous, marching *Whole Lotta Love*.

The album cover showed pictures of the band's heads superimposed over shots of First World War air aces while inside was a drawing of a Zeppelin captured in searchlight beams. This artwork by David Juniper resulted in one of Zep's simplest, yet most effective covers.

The engineering was by Eddie Kramer, George Chkiantz, Andrew Johns and Chris Huston. Even the overdubs sounded natural, with clever use of Robert's vocals ghosting in the background. Only the somewhat boomy bass guitar made *Whole Lotta Love* sound like a product of the times, otherwise the music was truly timeless. As Robert launched into the beautiful, almost Traffic-like *What Is And What Should Never Be*, the full range of his vocal style became apparent, making the 'phasing' and echo superfluous.

The relaxed dance band beat behind Jimmy's melodic solo was charming and contrasted brilliantly with the 'chugga chugga' rock breaks that climaxed the song. This sectionalised quality was typical of Zeppelin music, as the songs developed in a patchwork quilt fashion. Ideas were obviously shared between Jimmy, John Paul and Robert as the songs were put together in the studio, sometimes just starting with a drum beat and expanding over a period of days. Thus *The Lemon Song* began with a soul feel, raced away into a jazzy R&B rave up, then returned to semi-improvised blues choruses from Robert. It wasn't so different from the music played by dozens of British groups in the heyday of the small club circuit, but Zeppelin did it so much better than all the rest. And of course Robert's dissertation on the subject of his lemon seemed both daring and outrageous. Robert the balladeer made up for all this madness with *Thank You* the sort of song he most enjoyed working out, with suitably romantic organ backing from John Paul.

The heavier side of Zep was revealed on *Heartbreaker* with a typically

141

macho guitar and bass line locked in deadly embrace, humming menacingly behind Robert's vocal protests. Then came one of Jimmy's most stunning 'rock outs' on record, a series of solo breaks perfectly timed and played with savage intensity. The sudden stop to his solo was guaranteed to bring bursts of cheering at live gigs, and just as the idea of the theme began to wear thin, so the band segued into *Livin' Lovin' Maid* with the same neat dovetailing shown on the first album.

Some have pointed out the similarities between this riff and Gary Glitter's *I Didn't Know I Loved You (Till I Saw You Rock 'n' Roll)* hit of 1972. But then so many singers and bands took their cue from Zeppelin. John Bonham's *Moby Dick* drum solo was not particularly well recorded, a slightly muffled sound damping down the crack of his snare drum and the thunder of his tom toms. His attempt to recreate his stage drum solo in the studio didn't quite come off, but it remains a testament to the power of one of rock's greatest drummers; it's notable how much looser and zippier he got when the band returned for the final bars. All drummers need the excitement of a performance by the full band to inspire them.

Neither *Ramble On, Moby Dick* nor *Bring It On Home* were vintage Zeppelin, but the final cuts of *II* all had their moments, like the whining riff on *Home* which was and is irresistible. The final piping notes of Robert's harmonica signing off this album almost signalled that there would be some hard thinking about the next one, as if this was going to be goodnight to traditional blues. It could not remain Zeppelin fare for ever.

Led Zeppelin III, issued in 1970, began with *Immigrant Song* and I was in the studio when the backing track was laid down. I can remember seeing Bonzo hammering away at his kit while Jimmy casually launched into its distinctive riff, built around a kind of side-slipping bass drum beat. The new album with its curious revolving wheel cover had an atmosphere that was both brooding and mysterious. *Friends*, where the acoustic guitars shuffled over doomy chords suggested *Mars* from Holst's *Planet Suite*. By now Zeppelin were a massively successful band under the constant scrutiny of the world's press and audiences, and expected to produce endless miracles of rock 'n' roll. Their reaction was to branch out, experiment and play the thoughts and ideas that assailed them.

They were beyond merely impressing people with the cutting edge of metal, they were intent upon digging deep. The result was songs like the stomping, psychedelic *Celebration Day*, Robert shouting his message through a kind of mad folk dance.

One wonders what the reaction might have been among Atlantic record executives on hearing side two of *Zeppelin III* for the first time. Shock, consternation and dismay may well have been on the agenda, for

142

the music became increasingly uncompromising. *Gallows Pole* was fairly accessible as a folksy jig, with its frantic beat. *Tangerine* too was an attractive ballad performance by Robert which became a regular item at concerts. But *That's The Way, Bron-Y-Aur Stomp* and the final item *Hats Off To (Roy) Harper* showed increasing signs of madness. The latter item was described as being of traditional origin and arranged by 'Charles Obscure'. This was a new Zeppelin, reflective, romantic, and filled with the sound of banjos, twelve-string guitars and mandolins. Robert's lyrics about 'yesterday I saw you kissing tiny flowers' reflected the gangling poetical youth that lurks 'neath every rock 'n' roll rebel.

The skiffle-like rhythms of *Bron-Y-Aur Stomp* were familiar to those Britains who had grown up in the age of Lonnie Donegan, but there must have been many Zeppelin fans who were baffled by such material. And with the surreal *Hats Off* Zeppelin delivered a crushing riposte to all who felt they had the band figured out, in particular those critics who said you could only listen to their albums while stoned. This track consisted of Robert singing with a heavy tremelo effect like a Mullah calling the faithful to prayer, and Jimmy threatening his acoustic guitar with a kitchen knife or bottle neck. The guitar work was intense and the vocals well meaning if somewhat mannered. For those who yearned for the full band in action, the album boasted one of the finest Zeppelin performances of all time, *Since I've Been Loving You*, a rock blues which dripped emotion and has grown in stature with the years. The combination of *Loving You* and *Hats Off* tended to produce an imbalance, and *III* lacked the cohesiveness of the first two albums, but nevertheless it contained nuggets of pure gold and showed a band determined not to rest on its laurels.

The fourth album became known as *The Four Symbols* although it had no official title. It almost seemed as if the band were set to restore their role as purveyors of heavy rock with the first track *Black Dog*, which signalled thanks to fans for listening to the acoustic cuts of the previous album. On the other hand there may have been no more significance in such a heavy opening than that it was the way the material culled from various sessions fell together.

Even here the rock sound of Zeppelin in 1971 was appreciably different, perhaps more orthodox, particularly on *Rock And Roll* which was closer to the basic sound of Dave Edmunds' Rock Pile than *Dazed And Confused*. Bonzo set up a shuffle beat which propelled Robert's almost stately vocals at a brisk clip, but the lead guitar was rather too far back in the mix, with the bass guitar thrumming up front. On original Sun rock 'n' roll records, piano and lead guitar would have been much more prominent.

The late Sandy Denny, a fine singer and much loved, joined Robert for *The Battle Of Evermore* and they made an unexpectedly effective couple,

143

as the mandolins plunked a serenade to the tale of battles and castles. This was in effect a Robert Plant solo outing long before his career away from Zeppelin took shape. The Plantonian influence on Zeppelin music reached its apogee with the following track *Stairway To Heaven* a beautiful song by any standards and one of those 'lucky' melodies all composers dream about summoning from their innermost recesses.

The construction, with its pauses, twisting guitar melodies and almost reverential chords leading to John Bonham's delayed drum entrance, was masterful and inspired. Indeed, this one piece stands head and shoulders above the rest of the material on the album.

A kind of party atmosphere pervaded the cuts on side two, as if to rest and recuperate from the draining emotional experience of *Stairway To Heaven*. For example *Misty Mountain Hop* couldn't be simpler as a keyboard and guitar rocker, but even here there was something strange about the phrasing and 6/8 feel. A jolly yo ho, but as with all Zeppelin productions there was more beneath the surface to explore.

Another example of this was *Four Sticks*; separate tracks stuck together creating really a bit of a mess in which Robert's voice lost all its natural power, processed as in an electronic food mixer. There was a thin dividing line between a worthwhile experiment and failing to deliver the goods, and Zeppelin had begun to cross this divide with *Four Sticks*, chunks of which consist of Robert muttering 'ooh yeah' while drums and guitars persist with a fairly unrewarding theme.

Such surreal studio experiments were offset by a return to more orthodox singer-songwriter stuff with *Going To California*; Robert delved once more into tales of the 'wrath of the gods', in minstrel mode with 'la las' replacing 'baby babies'. This rather unconvincing item showed that a singer is often only as good as his song, and this wasn't up to scratch. A largely unrewarding side two was salvaged with *When The Levee Breaks*, John Bonham's powerful drumming cutting a swathe through all the 'la la' airy fairy nonsense and restoring some beef. But even this riff wasn't really vintage Zeppelin and it seemed they were treading water and even being careless, with some out of tune harmonica playing bum notes!

Even the most dedicated Zeppelin fans were beginning to grow uneasy after sitting through *Four Sticks* and *The Levee* and thus the fifth album *Houses Of The Holy* was approached with some trepidation. With the first cut, *The Song Remains The Same*, it seemed loyalty had been rewarded. It began in grand fashion with a superb guitar fanfare that promised much. Jimmy was tugging the band into a more positive direction with this song, but Robert persisted in singing like a mewling kitten with too much studio trickery cloaking his finest asset, his powerful, beautiful voice. Perhaps Robert felt he had given too much of his vocal technique away on the early albums and needed to find more

144

ways to impress by speeding up tapes. But in retrospect and indeed as I felt at the time, it was all unnecessary, like a great cellist playing inside a sack, or a painter painting blindfold.

Robert thankfully tore away the veil on *The Rain Song* which he delivered with restraint, while John Paul Jones experimented with a Mellotron - a now defunct instrument which sought to emulate an orchestra by mechanical means, using tape loops, before the advent of synthesisers. The overall effect was of some Sixties' pop session rather than a Led Zeppelin creation. Worse was to come with *The Crunge*, an ersatz soul opus with Robert rapping and talking nonsense in an irritating fashion. Then came *D'yer Mak'er* an excursion into reggae which I disliked on first hearing and have never liked since. And with *Dancing Days* they were in danger of just becoming another studio band with no sense of their own mission. Quite what was the cause of all these aberrations I have never been able to fathom, but at the time I reviewed the album with complaints that the band had become boring and lost their sense of direction.

John Bonham's raucous drumming which normally I loved with a passion, seemed totally at odds with the kind of subtlety required in reggae and Robert's mumbling and yelling was pure self-indulgence, forgiveable in a small club jam session but not capable of sustaining interest on a record. Fortunately the final tracks, *No Quarter* and *The Ocean*, went some way to making up for the weaker tracks, but it was many months before Zeppelin committed themselves to wax again, and when they returned, it was with a vengeance.

And so it was in 1975 that Zeppelin unleashed *Physical Graffiti*, a double album that at a stroke revitalised their recorded output. They sounded reborn from the opening bars of *Custard Pie*. The world-wide tightening up of rhythm sections in pop music, and the funky influence in disco was evident in Zep's crisp delivery. The sense of unity that had been slowly dissipated on the previous three albums returned and each did what he did best. The harmonica solos and improvised vocals over relentless riffs remained, but now they were held in check to keep each piece in focus.

The ambient sound was good, if not as electric as in days of yore, but at least there were fewer gimmicks and the guitars blew fresh and clean on *The Rover*, which sounded like an American rock song as performed by The Eagles or Bob Seger, with a nice middle eight. *In My Time Of Dying* roamed through many changing moods during eleven minutes of attacking music with some of Bonham's most aggressive ensemble playing.

Side Two saw a trio of show-stopping items, *Houses Of The Holy* followed by the astonishing *Trampled Underfoot* and the Eastern fantasy *Kashmir*. The power of these themes was rammed home when the band

145

played at Earls Court that year.

John Paul Jones' electric piano intro and backing riff to *Trampled Underfoot* made it a most untypical Zeppelin performance, closer in spirit to Stevie Wonder than *Communication Breakdown*, but it resulted in a new masterwork. Similarly *Kashmir* was out of character, but showed a positive new direction, vastly superior to the tentative casting about for inspiration that had marred their flawed fifth album. This was John Paul's baby and showed how the band benefitted when he exerted his presence.

This was richly satisfying rock by any standards and caused many to re-think their evaluation of the band.

The quasi-orchestral arrangement, *Kashmir*, was brilliantly conceived and executed. It shouted from the roof tops an exultant cry of triumph. Inspired by their travels in the East, *Kashmir* represented the peak of Zeppelin's musical achievements.

In The Light, which opened side three, was another broad musical canvas on which the band painted with bold strokes. A song of revelation, it suggested the born again faith of Zeppelin in themselves and their ability. It also pointed to deeper spiritual ideas, concepts and longings heightened in people made only too aware of the shallow nature of material rewards and values. A part of the hedonism of rock's more innocent, less practical age, it certainly induced a lot of fine music. And when the chips were down, Jimmy Page could always clear the air with a simple but perfect piece of unaccompanied acoustic guitar playing.

Bron-Y-Aur was such a two minute interlude, before Robert's relaxed journey into *Down By The Sea Side*. This wasn't so good, but provided relaxation between heavier items like *Ten Years Gone*.

Side four was generally less rewarding territory. *Night Flight* had slow, reticent electric organ backing behind Robert's busy, wordy vocals, while John's drums seemed to drag. This was an aberration. Only Robert seemed to be trying. Perhaps the aim was to reproduce the sound of a typical British organ based blues band of the Sixties. It added to the mystery of Zeppelin's decision making, not always governed by logic.

Jimmy harked, perhaps unconsciously, back to his session days, blowing the chunky motifs that launched a dozen hits. Of the remaining material *The Wanton Song* was workmanlike but undistinguished, while *Boogie With Stu* featured Rolling Stones man Ian Stewart guesting on what sounded like Winifred Atwell's 'other piano'. Ramshackle but fun. The same could be said of *Black Country Woman*, a duet between Robert and Jimmy with ferocious on-beat bass drumming. Back to the skiffle group and to hell with the platinum discs.

Sick Again, a song about life in LA made a suitable cohesive ending,

146

but the intriguing title showed more promise than the piece. *Physical Graffiti*, their first release on their own Swan Song label could have been issued as a single album and perhaps gained in impact, but in packing in odd bits of material it showed the band at work in various stages of concentration and moods. It was typical of them to appear so casual and makeshift at times and then blitz in with overwhelming power and perfection, so that the weakest items appeared all part of the plan.

The next album, *Presence*, was even more of a surprise. It came without much warning in 1976, just when the first stirrings of punk were being felt and the tide of opinion was turning against super-groups. It was recorded in Germany and everything from the cover art to the selection of songs seemed oddly different. Apart from a note on the spine of the album cover, there was no mention of the band's name and the cover shot was one of a selection of photographs dredged from the files of Hipgnosis and printed over with a shot of an 'object' more phallic than surreal. It was intended to depict Zeppelin's indefinable power.'

They may not have realised it, but Led Zeppelin were under colder scrutiny from unbelievers than ever before. New generations of record buyers, and critics had to be won over, and not by past reputation alone. But it is doubtful if such considerations impinged upon the group's collective psyche. Their concern was to go on getting out the music that seemed to well up within them whenever the old team got together.

The most important track on the album was the first one. *Achilles Last Stand* was a riproaring triumph and as inventive in its way as *Kashmir*, and as powerful as *Trampled Underfoot*. Once again Led Zeppelin had produced a kind of rock tone poem, a flood of emotion and fury.

There are many Achilles in history, from Achilles of Rome, who was tribune of the Roman plebs, to Achilles of The West and Achilles the hero of the Iliad. There was the Achilles who raced a tortoise and Achilles who was dipped in the Styx to be made invulnerable, but was slain by an arrow in his weak spot – the heel. Quite how Zeppelin's Achilles makes his last stand and to what purpose is not quite clear, but there are no signs of faltering or any weak spots in his armour. The piece raced along at furious tempo with cast iron constitution.

Such was the excitement of this session that Robert tripped over and injured his already damaged foot. Much of the pressure came from John Bonham's inspired drumming, a series of rolls and crashes which both goaded and punctuated the guitars in their headlong flight. Robert's vocals almost formed a narrative, while the whole arrangement had epic qualities. It was one of the last great works to be composed and per-formed by Zeppelin before they headed for extinction.

Its battering triplets formed by the bass and drums phrasing in unison created a tension and release sequence repeated throughout a remarkable series of choruses. This was sublime Zeppelin and anything afterwards was bound to be an anti-climax, as were songs like *For Your Life* which merely marked time. But being Zeppelin of course there were moments of interest and the band stomped with the clean sound obtained in the Musicland Studios in Munich.

Royal Orleans returned to the same sort of funky backbeat that Page and John Paul could rip out with ease and came complete with uncharacteristic choked hi-hat beats from Bonzo. Once again the tightness of the ensemble playing was in sharp contrast to the looseness of early Zeppelin and showed they kept their ear to the ground.

Nobody's Fault But Mine was undermined by some overlong pauses which dissipated the energy set up by a locomotive beat, but it reeked of *The New Yardbirds* when Robert got out his trusty old harmonica. It was a piece that belonged to 1968 but was played with the expertise of 1976. Perhaps this was due to the time warping effect of *The Object*.

Likewise, *Candy Store Rock* reproduced the sound of a Fifties teenage garage band, with lots of echo, tremelo, and Cliff Richard style 'yeahs' from Robert. Once again the excessive 'oohs' and 'baby yeah it's alright' sounded suspiciously like a drying up in the lyric writing department, but there are times when one 'yeah' is worth a thousand tales of Old Albion, and despite a strangely cold and clinical feel, *Candy Store Rock* and *Hots On For Nowhere* seemed to anticipate the arrival of later rock revivalists like The Stray Cats. The roundelay mode was surprisingly playful, not a mood one associates with Zeppelin, and all in all it was one of the strangest items they ever produced, notable for Bonzo's raunchy slop beat behind Jimmy's dancing guitar.

Tea For One, the closer, was a beautiful slow blues consisting of those simple, clean, crystal guitar notes all too often sacrificed on the altar of overdubs and the need to create a wall of sound. This was also one of Robert's best vocal performances on record for some while: free of gimmicks and flannel, and closer to the spirit of Paul Rodgers and Free. For a few glorious bars they could forget the burden of being Led Zeppelin, of making a new LP for the critics to devour, and simply play the music, the blues that had led them into the whole business in the first place. They should have put out a secret album of such material under a false name, just for the cognoscenti, and their own satisfaction. The unpressurised nature of *Tea For One* gave Jimmy the chance to extemporise in his most tasteful way.

Just a few months after *Presence* came another Zeppelin release, and a double album to boot. Zeppelin fans had never had such an embarrassment of riches, and this time they could hear the Zeppelin everyone knew and loved, 'live' in concert. It was of course the soundtrack of the movie *The Song Remains The Same* culled from a Madison Square concert.

148

It showed just how well the band played on those early Seventies concerts, and how much better than they had been in their 1969 period. The clarity and balance were perfect, and the reinterpretation of hits from past albums resulted in some stunning developments.

Notably, the title track contained some spirited guitar playing and there was an interplay between Bonham and Jones' bass not always appreciated during the hurly burly of a concert.

The band made a royal progress through its finest works, *Dazed And Confused*, *No Quarter*, *Stairway To Heaven*, *Moby Dick* and *Whole Lotta Love*. There was not much more that needs be said about these performances, except to note that they serve as a reminder of the pitch they played in those days. When the album was released, many felt there was no need to play it. It was possible to see the band play 'live' and hear the tunes at will. Now it takes on the significance of an action replay, an aural video of past events. Those who lived through them cannot quite believe they are gone forever. What was once taken for granted becomes increasingly precious. It is a relief to hear that Zeppelin 'live' really were as good as we thought. It wasn't all a mirage.

Two and a half years later came *In Through The Out Door* their last official studio album, issued in August 1979 and now fascinating for its glimpse of the way the band was going and its hints at a possible future. Recorded in Stockholm, it had even more intensity and definition than *Presence*. This became immediately apparent from the rocking *In The Evening*. While not as overwhelming as *Achilles Last Stand*, nevertheless it had a juggernaut's sense of momentum and one of those throat grabbing riffs that were Jimmy's forte. It was easy to talk about *A Whole Lotta Bluff*. If you set your mind against something, then all virtues become vices. Like Radio Moscow broadcasters, the critics were able to interpret the facts with a slant all of their own making. There was no bluff about Zeppelin's intentions with this album. Their contribution was just as valid as anybody else's within the musical spectrum.

With roots in the old song *Shaking All Over*, the new Zeppelin theme, *In The Evening* was one of those tunes any band would love to play all night. They had fun cutting it, and the mood was maintained on *South Bound Saurez*, where John Paul's boogie piano hustled a bar room beat. *Fool In The Rain* which followed, was released as a single in America where it was a hit. A Latin American foray, it had some remarkably nifty drumming. Bonzo was always at his best with a job to do and a tune to work on. Here he excelled, showing a grasp of a complex rhythmic feel new to the band.

The crescendo in the middle of *Fool* was such a pile up of emotions, you can almost hear the musicians falling over themselves with excitement. Jimmy inserted a jazz guitar solo to calm things for the return to Robert's vocal. On this album Plant showed a greater maturity, using

149

his range with great concern for the lyrical content and not just the sound of the words.

Hot Dog was a C&W hoe down that few ever expected to hear from Zeppelin which was a good enough reason for playing it. *Carouselambra* on side two was as close to modern techno pop as they ever got, an impression caused by John Paul's upfront keyboard work and the chanted vocals. An interesting piece, finely wrought and engineered with a difficult slowed-down section, *Carouselambra* was initially difficult to take, but on reappraisal it shows how Zeppelin's upward curve had begun again.

So continuous experiment went on and the results were varied. The achievement of *In Through The Out Door* was to sustain the attack. It wasn't rendered lopsided by the inclusion of one blockbuster and various remnants. Each piece was well fashioned and complete. There was no sloppiness or self-indulgence. Thus *All My Love* was a finely crafted song, beautifully sung, with some sympathetic keyboard playing to provide a suitable counterpoint to Jimmy's flowing chords. It was a sad song, a *Layla* for Zeppelin.

The final piece, *I'm Gonna Crawl* with its symphonic introduction, sounded as if it might be a theme by Elgar, but turned instead into a stunning work-out for Robert, a slow soul drama, dealing with the strains of love's demands. It was also a bow to James Brown, but the notes and the mood was all Zeppelin.

A particularly telling moment came when Jimmy Page launched in his solo after some tender synthesiser. The song faded out like a movie, sinking into the sunset amid rolling credits.

Coda was the last album (thus far), released in 1982, and oddly enough the first title was *We're Gonna Groove* (as opposed to crawl), and this went right back to the earliest days, when the group were in Morgan Studios, London in 1969. It was a Ben E. King song, and not so far removed from the spirit of *I'm Gonna Crawl* which showed how Robert held some things dear in his musical memory. With many groups, items from the archives are an embarrassment, showing just how badly everything was played and produced in the good old days. Not so with Zeppelin. There were differences in tone and attack, but the power and quality was always there.

The album, produced by Jimmy, and released two years after the end of the band, was an instructive mix of material which showed there was never a period when the band weren't looking about for new sources of inspiration.

Poor Tom, an oddity from 1970 had Robert reciting what sounded like a nursery rhyme over a Bonham shuffle beat which in itself was a lesson in co-ordination and drum rudiments. It just showed the strange things they got up to in the studio at times.

150

Even more exciting was a version of *I Can't Quit You Baby*, actually recorded during a sound check at the Royal Albert Hall in 1970 with the aid of a mobile truck. The ambience of the empty hall was perfect and resulted in an even better version of the tune than was issued on the first album. Fortunately for posterity someone had the good sense to keep this intact.

Walter's Walk from 1972 was distinguished by angry Page breaks, a brutal snare and bass drum beat and somewhat mechanical echo on Plant's voice. A charmless episode, and *Ozone Baby* which followed, on side two, was much better.

This came from the same Polar Studios, Stockholm which had been home to *In Through The Out Door* and had the same engineer at work, Leif Masses. The sound achieved was as fresh as a sauna bath and Robert's singing as lively as a session in a jacuzzi.

The same excellence prevailed on *Darlene* from the same 1978 sessions and was recorded a couple of days later on November 16. This was a raunchy teen ballad with solo breaks from piano and guitar in the true spirit of *Go Man, Go*. It broke into a boogie shuffle that was pure pub rock in the style of Chas'n'Dave.

Jimmy back tracked two years in his search through the archives for *Bonzo's Montreux* which showcased *The John Bonham Drum Orchestra*. It consisted of John improvising a solo around a solid, heavy beat á la Sandy Nelson. Various electronics were employed to enhance the sound and obtain a melody of sorts.

John was rather ill-served by his drum solos on record. None did him justice. The best solos I ever heard him play were out on the road. For example, I never heard him play so fast and with such a free flow of ideas as he did at Carnegie Hall in New York. Later on, with the burden of a nightly solo to unleash, he tended to over extend himself and play into a corner. His best work was always as part of the band, helping the creative process on *Achilles Last Stand* or on *Fool In The Rain*.

The last item, *Wearing And Tearing*, also came from the Stockholm tapes and was a small earthquake – with not many injured. Pauses graced by heavy accents were designed to give Robert room to strut his stuff, and his frantic chanting over a series of resounding chords was like The Police (then an up and coming band) on speed.

There must be more archive material available, gathering dust in boxes, that will one day see the light, although *Coda*, in the meantime, fulfilled the promise Jimmy once made, when Zeppelin were off the road, to bring out a record that would be a chronological history of the band.

Until then the ten Zeppelin albums already available for our inspection, are their own testament, and will remain a constant source of delight.

151

DISCOGRAPHY

Singles (American Releases Only)

Date	Title	Catalogue No.
March 1969	Good Times, Bad Times/ Communication Breakdown	Atlantic 2613
November 1969	Whole Lotta Love/Livin' Lovin' Maid	Atlantic 2690
November 1970	Immigrant Song/Hey Hey What Can I Do	Atlantic 2777
December 1971	Black Dog/Misty Mountain Hop	Atlantic 2849
March 1972	Rock And Roll/Four Sticks	Atlantic 2865
May 1973	Over The Hills And Far Away/ Dancing Days	Atlantic 2970
October 1973	D'yer Mak'er/The Crunge	Atlantic 2986
March 1975	Trampled Underfoot/Black Country Woman	Swan Song 70102
May 1976	Candy Store Rock/Royal Orleans	Swan Song 70110
December 1979	Fool In The Rain/Hot Dog	Swan Song 71003

N.B. Trampled Underfoot/Black Country was released in a rare promotional edition in the U.K. in March 1975. 10,000 copies were pressed which now sell at £10 each among collectors. No other official Led Zeppelin singles were released in the U.K.

152

Albums

Date	Title	Catalogue No.
March 1969	LED ZEPPELIN Good Times Bad Times/Babe I'm Gonna Leave You/You Shook Me/Dazed And Confused/Your Time Is Gonna Come/Black Mountain Side/Communication Breakdown/I Can't Quit You Baby/How Many More Times	Atlantic K 40031
October 1969	LED ZEPPELIN II Whole Lotta Love/What Is And What Should Never Be/The Lemon Song/Thank You/Heartbreaker/Living Loving Maid (She's Just A Woman)/Ramble On/Moby Dick/Bring It On Home	Atlantic K 40037
October 1970	LED ZEPPELIN III Immigrant Song/Friends/Celebration Day/Since I've Been Loving You/Out On The Tiles/Gallows Pole/Tangerine/That's The Way/Bron-Y-Aur Stomp/Hats Off To (Roy) Harper	Atlantic K 50002
November 1971	FOUR SYMBOLS Black Dog/Rock And Roll/The Battle Of Evermore/Stairway To Heaven/Misty Mountain Hop/Four Sticks/Going To California/When The Levee Breaks	Atlantic K 50008
March 1973	HOUSES OF THE HOLY The Song Remains The Same/The Rain Song/Over The	Atlantic K 50014

Hills And Far Away/The
Crunge/Dancing Days/D'yer
Mak'er/No Quarter/The
Ocean

March 1975   PHYSICAL GRAFFITI   Swan Song SSK 89400
Custard Pie/The Rover/In My
Time Of Dying/Houses Of
The Holy/Trampled
Underfoot/Kashmir/In The
Light/Bron-Y-Aur/Down By
The Seaside/Ten Years Gone/
Night Flight/The Wanton
Song/Boogie With Stu/Black
Country Woman/Sick Again

April 1976   PRESENCE   Swan Song SSK 59402
Achilles Last Stand/For Your
Life/Royal Orleans/
Nobody's Fault But Mine/
Candy Store Rock/Hots On
For Nowhere/Tea For One

October 1976   THE SONG REMAINS   Swan Song SSK 89402
THE SAME
Rock And Roll/Celebration
Day/The Song Remains The
Same/Rain Song/Dazed And
Confused/No Quarter/
Stairway To Heaven/Moby
Dick/Whole Lotta Love

August 1979   IN THROUGH THE   Swan Song SSK 59410
OUT DOOR
In The Evening/South Bound
Saurez/Fool In The Rain/Hot
Dog/Carouselambra/All My
Love/I'm Gonna Crawl

1982   CODA   Swan Song A0051
We're Gonna Groove/Poor
Tom/I Can't Quit You Baby/
Walter's Walk/Ozone Baby/
Darlene/Bonzo's Montreux/
Wearing And Tearing

154

SELECTION OF BOOTLEG ALBUMS

Title	*Label*

JAMES PATRICK PAGE SESSION MAN   Creative Artistry
Diamonds/Somebody Told My Girl/The
Feminist Look/Talking About You/Roll Over
Beethoven/Money Honey/That's Alright/My
Baby Left Me/Leave My Kitten Alone/A Certain
Girl/Don't You Dig This Kinda Beat/Once In A
While/Night Comes Down/Little By Little/I Just
Can't Go To Sleep/She Just Satisfies/Keep
Movin'/Is It True/Leaves Come Tumbling
Down/Get A Load Of This/You Said/How Do
You Feel/Surprise, Surprise/Hot House Of
Omagarashid/I'm Confused/Garden Of My
Mind/You're The One/Just Like Anyone Would
Do/Zoom Widge & Wag/Bald Headed Woman

LED ZEPPELIN LIVE AT THE LYCEUM
IN LONDON 1969   Grant Musik
Good Times, Bad Times/Communication
Breakdown/I Can't Quit You/Heartbreaker/You
Shook Me/What Is And What Should Never Be/
How Many More Times /Eyesight To The Blind/
Let That Boy Boogie Woogie.

LIVE IN JAPAN – A CELLARFUL OF NOISE   Fliedlice Records
Tangerine/Moby Dick/Celebration Day/
Immigrant Song/Heartbreaker/Stairway To
Heaven

BALLCRUSHER   Flat
Immigrant Song/Heartbreaker/Since I've Been
Loving You/Black Dog/That's The Way/The
Lemon Song/Whole Lotta Love/
Communication Breakdown/Going To
California/Dazed And Confused

BBC BROADCAST 1971   TMOQ
Communication Breakdown/Dazed And
Confused/Going To California/Stairway To
Heaven/What Is And What Should Never Be/

Medley: Whole Lotta Love, Boogie Woogie,
That's Alright Mama, Stop What's That Sound,
Minnesota Blues

EARL'S COURT 1975   Europe
No Quarter/Tangerine/Kashmir/Going To
California/That's The Way/Woodstock

EARL'S COURT 11   Europe
In My Time Of Dying/The Song Remains The
Same/Trampled Underfoot/Black Dog/Stairway
To Heaven

FOR BADGE HOLDERS ONLY   Dragonfly Records
Sick Again/Nobody's Fault But Mine/Over The
Hills And Far Away/Since I've Been Loving
You/Ten Years Gone/The Battle Of Evermore/
Going To California/Black Mountain Side/
Kashmir/Trampled Underfoot/Stairway To
Heaven/Medley: Whole Lotta Love, Rock And
Roll

FOR BADGE HOLDERS ONLY: PART TWO   K&S
No Quarter/Black Country Woman/Out On The
Tiles/Moby Dick/Star Spangled Banner/Achilles
Last Stand

KNEBWORTH FAIR VOLUME ONE   K&S
Communication Breakdown/I Can't Quit You/
Dazed And Confused/What Is And What Should
Never Be/Communication Breakdown/My
Rider/Whole Lotta Love/I Can't Quit You/White
Summer/The Song Remains The Same/
Celebration Day/Black Dog/Nobody's Fault But
Mine/Over The Hills And Fair Away/Misty
Mountain Hop

KNEBWORTH FAIR: VOLUME TWO   K&S
Since I've Been Loving You/Rain Song/Sick
Again/White Summer/Black Mountain Side/
Kashmir/Trampled Underfoot/Guitar & Drum
Solo/In The Evening/Stairway To Heaven/Rock
And Roll/Whole Lotta Love/Heartbreaker

LIVE AT KNEBWORTH AUGUST 4, 1979 PART TWO
Kashmir/Trampled Underfoot/Rain Song/
White Summer/Black Mountain Side/Stairway
To Heaven/Whole Lotta Love/Heartbreaker/
Rock And Roll/Hot Dog/Achilles Last Stand

SOLO ALBUMS

JIMMY PAGE

Death Wish II Original Soundtrack   Swan Song SSK 59415

ROBERT PLANT

| June 1982 | Pictures At Eleven | Swan Song SSK 59418. |
| June 1983 | The Principle Of Moments | Atlantic 79-0101-1 |

THE BEST IN ROCK 'N' ROLL READING
Bestselling rock references

A-Z OF ROCK SINGERS
by John Tobler

The third volume in the highly acclaimed A-Z of Rock reference series, this book turns the spotlight onto the greatest singers in the first 25 years of rock 'n' roll. Over 250 singers whose distinctive styles, songs and personalities stand out as landmarks of rock history are profiled. Presented in encyclopedic form, each entry contains career background, an assessment of the singer's best work and selected discographies.

128 pages: 60 black/white photos. 8 pages of colour. Selected discographies.
ISBN: 0 86276 139 5 p/b

A-Z OF ROCK GUITARISTS
by Chris Charlesworth

A companion in the A-Z of Rock reference series, this book brings together the techniques and styles, personalities, classic cuts and performances of over 200 of the world's greatest rock guitarists and bass players.

128 pages: 120 black/white photos. 8 pages of colour. Index and select discographies.
ISBN: 0 86276 080 1 p/b

A-Z OF ROCK DRUMMERS
by Harry Shapiro

Part of the popular A-Z of Rock reference series, this book focuses on the over 200 drummers who have given the beat to rock 'n' roll from the sixties to the present, from the legendary Ginger Baker to Stewart Copeland of the Police.

128 pages: 120 black/white photos and 8 pages of colour. Index and select discographies.
ISBN: 0 86276 084 4 p/b

ROCK HERITAGE: THE SIXTIES
by Chris Charlesworth

The first volume in a trilogy on the history of rock 'n' roll, this book features a 20,000-word commentary on international developments of the most tumultuous decade in pop music, portraits of the musicians, songwriters and industry personalities in the vanguard of the rock revolution, a ten-year chronology, and a comprehensive survey of the charts, concerts, festivals and songs that were the sixties.

160 pages: 70 black/white photos. 16 pages colour. Select discography.
ISBN: 0 86276 131 X p/b

THE PERFECT COLLECTION
Edited by Tom Hibbert

The ultimate rock list book – 200 albums to have on a desert island.

96 pages: 100 black/white photos.
ISBN: 0 86276 105 0 p/b

RARE RECORDS
by Tom Hibbert

In-depth information on little known masterpieces and the record collecting trade. A must for all collectors.

128 pages: 50 colour and black/white photos.
ISBN: 0 86276 047 X p/b

PROTEUS
ROCKS

The Best Rock 'n' Roll Reading from Proteus

OYAH
n illustrated fan's eyeview
uch-liked by Toyah herself.
y Gaynor Evans
K £1.95
S $3.95

**EGGAE: DEEP
OOTS MUSIC**
he definitive history of reggae.
major TV tie-in.
y Howard Johnson and Jim
nes
K £5.95
S $10.95

OOKENDS
he first full study of Simon
nd Garfunkel, their joint and
lo careers.
y Patrick Humphries
K £5.95
S $10.95

RETENDERS
he first full study of this
owerful and turbulent band.
y Chris Salewicz
K £3.95
S $7.95

OU REED
definitive profile of this
most reclusive figure.
y Diana Clapton
K £4.95
S $9.95.

AMES LAST
A fully illustrated study of this
orld phenomenon of
opular music.
y Howard Elson
K £4.95
S $9.95

RARE RECORDS
complete illustrated guide
wax trash and vinyl
reasures.
y Tom Hibbert
K £4.95
S $9.95

**HE PERFECT
COLLECTION**
he 200 greatest albums, the
00 greatest singles selected
nd discussed by leading rock
urnalists.
dited by Tom Hibbert
K £4.95
S $9.95

ARLY ROCKERS
ll the seminal figures of rock
n' roll:
erry, Little Richard, Jerry Lee,
resley et al.
y Howard Elson
JK £4.95
JS $9.95

order form overleaf

KATE BUSH ☐
Complete illustrated story of
this unique artist.
by Paul Kerton
UK £3.95
US $7.95

BLACK SABBATH ☐
Heavy Metal Superstars.
by Chris Welch
UK £4.95
US $9.95

**A-Z OF ROCK
GUITARISTS** ☐
First illustrated encyclopaedia
of guitar greats.
by Chris Charlesworth
UK £5.95
US $10.95

**A-Z OF ROCK
DRUMMERS** ☐
Over 300 great drummers in
this companion to ROCK
GUITARISTS.
by Harry Shapiro
UK £5.95
US $10.95

CHUCK BERRY ☐
The definitive biography of
the original Mr Rock 'n' Roll.
by Krista Reese
UK £4.95
US $8.95

**A CASE OF
MADNESS** ☐
A big illustrated guide for
fans of this insane band.
by Mark Williams
UK only £1.95

TALKING HEADS ☐
The only illustrated book
about one of the most
innovative bands of the 70s
and 80s.
by Krista Reese
UK £4.95
US $9.95

DURAN DURAN ☐
The best-selling illustrated
biography.
UK £1.95
US $3.95

**A TOURIST'S GUIDE
TO JAPAN** ☐
Beautifully illustrated study
of Sylvian and his colleagues.
by Arthur A. Pitt.
UK £1.95
US $3.95

**ILLUSTRATED
POP QUIZ** ☐
Over 400 impossible questions
for pop geniuses only.
by Dafydd Rees and Barry
Lazell
UK £2.95
US $5.95